Evaluating Viewpoints:
Critical Thinking in United States History Series

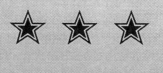

BOOK THREE
RECONSTRUCTION
TO
PROGRESSIVISM

KEVIN O'REILLY

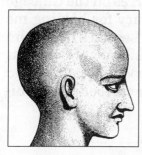

© 1983, 1991
CRITICAL THINKING BOOKS & SOFTWARE
www.criticalthinking.com
P.O. Box 448 • Pacific Grove • CA 93950-0448
Phone 800-458-4849 • FAX 831-393-3277
ISBN 0-89455-417-4
Printed in the United States of America
Reproduction rights granted for single-classroom use only.

ABOUT THE AUTHOR

Kevin O'Reilly is a social studies teacher at Hamilton-Wenham Regional High School in Massachusetts. He was named by *Time* magazine and the National Council for the Social Studies as the 1986 Outstanding Social Studies Teacher in the United States. In addition to these four volumes on Critical Thinking in United States History, Mr. O'Reilly is the coauthor of *Critical Viewing: Stimulant to Critical Thinking* (also published by Midwest Publications/Critical Thinking Press & Software) and the author of "Escalation," a computer simulation on the Vietnam War (Kevin O'Reilly, 6 Mason Street, Beverly, MA 01915). Mr. O'Reilly, who has a Master of Arts Degree in History, is an editor of the *New England Journal of History*. He conducts workshops throughout the United States on critical thinking, critical viewing, and decision-making.

> **FOR**
> My sons
> Brian and Sean

ACKNOWLEDGMENTS

I would like to thank the following for their help: Gordon Library for helping me track down sources on the Chicago Stockyards (Lesson 17); Beverly Library for helping me research the Fourteenth Amendment (Lesson 6) and John D. Rockefeller (Lesson 15 and 16); the Library of Congress for finding numerous pictures for the book (Lessons 9 and 17); and Historical Pictures Service for cartoons on immigration (Lesson 26).

TABLE OF CONTENTS

INTRODUCTION

Thinking is what history is all about, as we try to more fully understand our past and thereby ourselves. We don't have many answers in history. Instead, we search for the truth, always attempting to get closer to what really happened. This book is meant to give you a taste of the excitement of historical interpretation and debate. It is also meant to give you guidance in learning the skills necessary to evaluate conflicting viewpoints. The goal is to empower you, as citizens in a democratic society, to make decisions for yourself regarding what you read, see, or hear about the issues of tomorrow—issues where there are few easy answers, and where reasonable people disagree.

This book is about historical interpretations or viewpoints. It is not itself a history book, but rather a series of situations on which historians present differing opinions. The purpose of this book is to teach you how to analyze and evaluate historical arguments.

If you think of a social, political, or economic issue today, you'll realize that people approach problems with different viewpoints. For example, reasonable people disagree about how much money should be spent on social welfare programs, about how to fight crime, and about the best candidate in an election. Historians also disagree about many events in history. Just as there are different ways to tell a fictional story, so there are many ways to tell the story of history. Historians, depending upon their backgrounds and frames of reference, select different information as important or unimportant.

The root word of history is story. As a "story," history seeks to explain past events. Why did a particular event happen when it did? How did a particular person or group of people affect the world around them? What underlying forces shaped events? Good historians have taken the time to step back, to carefully examine events to see the whole picture more clearly, to explain events more fully, and, thereby, to help our understanding of the world.

There are two broad kinds of history: analytical and narrative. In analytical history a historian makes a strong argument about an issue. The thesis is obvious, and the rest of the interpretation consists of a series of arguments to support the thesis. You probably have written thesis/support arguments in your English or social studies classes.

The second kind of history is narrative. Here, the historian tells a story, usually in chronological order. The various elements of the situation—economic forces, technological changes, social institutions, personalities, and so forth—are brought together as the drama unfolds. The main argument or thesis is not always obvious in narrative history. It has to be inferred from the way the story is told. Nevertheless, narrative history also contains a point of view or a thesis about why events happened the way they did.

This book presents both analytical and narrative history. For example, the interpretations on Reconstruction in Lesson 7 are narrative; the interpretations in Lesson 25 are analytical; most are a combination of both.

©1991 Midwest Publications/Critical Thinking Press & Software, P.O. Box 448, Pacific Grove, CA 93950

One of the most important goals of this book is to introduce you to the conflicting viewpoints or interpretations of history. Ideally, you would read various historical interpretations of events, some of which are listed on pages 195–97. Realistically, you don't have the time to read all of these historical works. So this book contains short summaries of the interpretations. In some cases 300-page books have been summarized into one or two pages. Since this isn't fair to the original historians, their names have been replaced by titles: Historian A, Historian B, and so forth.

In some lessons the viewpoints are entitled Interpretation A or Theory A, rather than Historian A. Interpretation or Theory is used when no particular historian is identified with that point of view. These terms are also used to convey the idea that you should be forming your own interpretations or theories. The dictionary defines interpretation as "an explanation of what is not immediately plain or obvious," and it defines theory as "a judgment based on evidence or analysis." Ask your science teacher how the term *theory* is defined in science.

While most arguments presented in this book are those expressed by historians, a few are from historical participants. Thus, there are arguments by Andrew Carnegie and William Graham Sumner on the question of laissez-faire (Lesson 14).

This student book is comprised of three components:

Guide to Critical Thinking explains the parts of an argument and how to evaluate those parts.

Worksheets provide practice in the skills necessary for evaluating and constructing arguments.

Historical interpretation problems provide the opportunity for you to analyze historical arguments and make up your own mind.

Lessons within the book are arranged into three units: Reconstruction (Lessons 1–9), Industrialization and Response (Lessons 10–18), and Workers, Immigrants, and Farmers in the Late 1800s (Lessons 19–27).

Thirteen of the lessons (#1–5, 10–13, and 19–22) are short worksheet lessons which focus on practicing particular skills. The other fourteen lessons (#6–9, 14–18, and 23–27) are longer historical interpretation problems where the skills can be applied.

UNIT 1
GUIDE TO CRITICAL THINKING

Purpose of This Unit

This Guide is meant to help you improve your critical thinking skills. Critical thinking, as used in this book, means evaluating or judging arguments. The critical thinker asks, "Why should I believe this?" or "How do I know this is true?" Just as importantly, critical thinking means constructing good arguments. Here, the critical thinker asks, "Why do I believe this?" and "Do I have a logical, well-supported case to back up my claims?"

As mentioned in the Introduction to this text, you are going to be confronted in this book with opposing viewpoints. You will have to decide for yourself which are stronger and which are weaker. This Guide will help you with the critical thinking skills necessary to judge the viewpoints presented and to express your own verbal and written views on topics.

Historians use critical thinking skills constantly in evaluating the reliability of documents, in selecting what is important, and in determining the underlying causes for events. But critical thinking is useful in everyday life as well. It is called for in such situations as buying a car, watching the news, voting, or deciding on a job or career. Improved skills in this area will help you make better judgments more often.

You can get an overall picture of critical thinking by reading through this Guide. You will find it most useful, however, when you need to use a particular skill in a particular lesson. For example, the section on evaluating **Generalizations** will be useful in Lesson 9, which asks several questions on recognizing and drawing good generalizations.

When Is an Argument Not a Fight?

An *argument* or interpretation, as used in this Guide, refers to presenting a conclusion and defending it with reasons that logically lead to the conclusion. You will have to decide for yourself how strong each argument is. A *case* is a set of arguments. The strength of a case may be judged by examining individual arguments. Arguments or interpretations may include any or all of the following components.

• Assertions • Evidence • Reasoning •
• Assumptions • Values •

Keep the importance of words in mind as you look through the following pages. Words are the keys to arguments. Signal words like "but," "however," and "on the other hand" indicate a change of direction in an argument. Words will serve as your clues in identifying parts of an argument and, once the argument has been identified, they will serve as your keys in analyzing the strength of that argument.

Once you recognize an argument, you will want to analyze it. You will break it down into its respective parts and evaluate the elements against certain standards of excellence in reasoning and evidence. You will examine the assumptions to see if they are warranted. You will consider how the author's values shape the evidence and reasoning presented.

Assertions

An assertion is a statement, conclusion, main point, or claim concerning an issue, person, or idea. It can be the conclusion of a very short argument, or it can be the main point (thesis) of an argument of perhaps two or more paragraphs.

For example, consider the short argument, "Bob is very responsible, so I'm sure he'll show up." The conclusion (assertion) in the argument is the phrase "...so I'm sure he'll show up." (The part of the argument that isn't the conclusion ["Bob is very responsible,..."] is called the premise. Premises are assumptions or reasons offered to support a conclusion. See the section on **Assumptions**, pages 15–16.)

IDENTIFYING ASSERTIONS

Words that often cue an assertion or conclusion include "therefore," "then," "so," and "thus." You can also identify an assertion by asking yourself, "What is the author trying to prove? Of what is the author trying to convince me?"

EVALUATING ASSERTIONS

Two important questions to ask to evaluate the overall assertion of an argument are:

- Is the assertion supported by good reasons (supporting arguments)?
- Are the reasons supported by evidence?

Evidence

Evidence consists of the information a person uses to support assertions. It is the data, information, and knowledge which a historian, social scientist, or any communicator uses to support an argument; it is not the argument or interpretation itself.

There are many sources of evidence. Some of the more common sources include statements by witnesses or other people, written documents, objects, photographs, and video recordings. Lack of sources for evidence seriously weakens an argument. That is why many historical works include footnotes to cite sources; that is also why you should cite sources in essays you write.

For example, historians studying a Civil War battle could gather written accounts of the battle from sources such as diaries, battle reports, and letters. They could examine objects that had been found on the battlefield and photographs taken at the time of the battle. They also might use accounts by other historians, but these would be weaker sources because they are not eyewitness accounts (see primary sources below).

IDENTIFYING EVIDENCE

To help locate evidence in an argument, look for endnotes, quotation marks, or such words as "according to," "so-and-so said," or "such-and-such shows."

The initial questions to be asked when evaluating any evidence offered in support of an argument should be:
- Is there a source given for this information?
- If so, what is it?

EVALUATING EVIDENCE

Only when you know the sources of evidence can you judge how reliable the evidence actually is. Frequently, you can use the following evaluation method when considering evidence and its sources. This can be shortened to **PROP**; remember that good sources will "prop up" evidence.

P	Is it a primary (eyewitness) or secondary (not an eyewitness) source?
	Primary sources are invariably more desirable. To reach valid conclusions, you need to realize the importance of primary sources and gather as many as possible to use as evidence in an argument. You should depend on secondary sources, like encyclopedias or history texts, only when primary sources are unavailable.
R	If the source is a person, does he or she have any reason to distort the evidence?
	Would those giving the statement, writing the document, recording the audio (or video), or identifying the object benefit if the truth were distorted, covered up, falsified, sensationalized, or manipulated? Witnesses with no reason to distort the evidence are more desirable than those who might benefit from a particular presentation of the evidence.
O	Are there other witnesses, statements, recordings, or evidence which report the same data, information, or knowledge?
	Having other evidence verify the initial evidence strengthens the argument.
P	Is it a public or private statement?
	If the person making the statement of evidence knew or intended that other people should hear it, then it is a public statement. A private statement may be judged more accurate because it was probably said in confidence and is, therefore, more likely to reflect the speaker's true feelings or observations.

These four factors (**PROP**) will be enough to evaluate most evidence you encounter. Additional factors that are sometimes considered regarding evidence include:

Witnesses

- What are the frames of reference (points of view) of the witnesses? What are their values? What are their backgrounds?
- Are the witnesses expert (recognized authorities) on what they saw?
- Did the witnesses believe their statements could be checked? (If I believe you can check my story with other witnesses, I am more likely to tell the truth.)
- Was what the witnesses said an observation ("Maria smiled") or an inference ("Maria was happy")? Inferences are judgments that can reveal much about the witnesses' points of view or motives (reasons) for making statements.

Observation Conditions

- Were physical conditions conducive to witnessing the event? (Was it foggy? Noisy? Dark?)
- What were the physical locations of the witnesses in relation to the event? Were they close to the action? Was there anything blocking their view?

Witnesses' Statement or Document

- Is the document authentic or a forgery?
- What is the reputation of the source containing the document?
- How soon after the event was the statement made?
- Did the witnesses use precise techniques or tools to report or record the event? For example, did they take notes or use reference points?

Reasoning

Just as evidence can be judged for its reliability, so reasoning can be evaluated for its logic.

Reasoning is the logical process through which a person reaches conclusions. For example, you notice that the car is in the driveway (evidence) so you reason that your mother is home (conclusion). Five kinds of reasoning are frequently used in historical interpretations:
- cause and effect
- comparison
- generalization
- proof (by evidence, example, or authority)
- debating (eliminating alternatives)

These types of reasoning, along with questions to help evaluate them and fallacies (errors in reasoning) for each, are explained below.

Reasoning by Cause and Effect

This type of reasoning is used when someone argues that something caused, brought about, or will result in something else. For example, Laura's motorcycle will not start (effect), so she decides it must be out of gas (proposed cause).

Causation is very complex—so complex that some historians feel that they do not really understand the causes of an event even after years of study. Other historians do not even use the word cause; instead they talk about change. Please keep a sense of humility when you study causation. When you finish your course, you are not going to know all the causes of complex events. Rather, you are going to know a little bit more about how to sort out causes.

Historians believe in multiple causation, that is, that every event has several or many causes. This belief does not, however, relieve us of the responsibility of trying to figure out which are the most important causes. Indeed, one of the most frequent sources of debate among historians stems from disagreements over the main causes of events.

IDENTIFYING CAUSE-AND-EFFECT REASONING

One way to identify cause-and-effect reasoning is to watch for such cue words as "caused," "led to," "forced," "because," "brought about," "resulted in," or "reason for." You can also identify it by asking, "Is the author arguing that one thing resulted from another?"

EVALUATING CAUSE-AND-EFFECT REASONING

Several important questions may be used to evaluate the strength of a causal explanation.

- Is there a **reasonable connection** between the cause and the effect? Does the arguer state the connection?

  In the motorcycle example, for instance, there is a reasonable connection between the motorcycle being out of gas and not starting. Lack of gasoline would cause a motorcycle not to start.

- Might there be **other possible causes** for this effect? Has the arguer eliminated these as possible causes?

  There are also, however, other possible causes for a motorcycle failing to start. Maybe the starter isn't working. Other possible causes have not been eliminated.

- Might there be **important previous causes** that led to the proposed cause?

  In some cases a previous cause might be more important than the proposed cause; e.g., a leak in the gasoline tank might cause a motorcycle to be out of gasoline. In this case simply putting gasoline in the tank will not make the engine run again.

Cause-and-Effect Fallacies

Single cause

Any conclusion that a historical event had but one cause commits the single-cause fallacy. For example, the statements "Eloise married Jon because he's handsome" and "Antiwar protest caused the United States to pull out of the Vietnam War" both make use of the single-cause fallacy.

In both cases there are likely to be other factors, or causes, involved. The fallacy can be avoided by carefully investigating and explaining the complexity of causes. Be careful, however. Historians may sometimes assert that something "caused" an event when they really mean it was the main, not the only, cause.

Preceding event as cause

A Latin phrase (*Post hoc, ergo propter hoc*), meaning "after this, therefore because of this," is the technical name of a fallacy that occurs when someone assumes that because event B happened after event A, A caused B. "I washed my car, so naturally it rained" and "Since the Depression followed the stock market crash of 1929, the stock market crash must have caused it" are both examples of this fallacy. To avoid the error, the author of the argument must explain how A caused B.

Correlation as cause

This fallacy occurs when a conclusion is reached that because A and B occurred at the same time or occur regularly at the same time (the correlation), then one caused the other.

Some correlations, such as cigarette smoking and increased incidence of heart disease, are very strong. Others are not as strong. In some correlations where A is argued to cause B, ask yourself if B could instead have caused A. For example, "Students who have fewer absences (A) achieve higher grades in school (B)." In this case, consideration might also be given to the correlation that "Students who achieve higher grades in school (B) have fewer absences (A)."

Again, the fallacy might be avoided by an explanation of how A caused B. Since, however, a connection cannot always be shown, people are frequently forced to rely on correlations. For example, you don't have to know, mechanically, *how* a car works to know that turning the ignition should cause it to start.

False scenario

This fallacy uses the argument that if something had happened, then something else would have happened (or if something had not happened, then something else would not have happened). "If you hadn't told Mother on me, I wouldn't be in trouble" is an example of false-scenario reasoning. "If we had not built railroads in the late 1800s, the United States would not have had as much economic growth as it did with the railroads" is another.

Although some of this kind of predicting can occur when we have a great deal of evidence regarding what might have happened, it is generally much less certain than causal reasoning about what actually did happen. To avoid this fallacy, concern yourself with what actually happened rather than what might have happened.

Reasoning by Comparison

This type of reasoning, sometimes called "reasoning by analogy," consists of two basic types, both of which involve drawing comparisons between two cases.

Alike comparison

The first type of comparison chooses two cases (people, events, objects, etc.) and reasons that since they are alike in some ways, they will be alike in some other way. For example, Joe might reason that Fernandez did all his homework and got an "A" in geometry, so if Joe does all of his homework he can also get an "A." Joe is reasoning that since the two cases (his and Fernandez's) are similar in terms of homework (doing it all), they will be similar in terms of outcome (an "A").

Difference comparison

The second type compares two cases and reasons that since they are different in some respect, something must be true. For example, Juan might reason that his baseball team is better than Cleon's, since Juan's team won more games. Juan is concluding that since the two cases (teams) are different in some respect (one team won more games), it is true that the team that won the most games is a better team.

If Joe and Fernandez are taking the same course (geometry), and have the same mathematical ability and the same teacher, then the conclusion that the outcome would be the same is stronger than it would be if they were different in any or all of these areas. If the two baseball teams played the same opponents and the same number of games, then the conclusion that one team is better (different) than the other is stronger than it would be if they were different in any of these ways.

Usually, more similarities make a stronger argument. A similarity found in an argument of difference, however, will weaken the argument. If the two baseball teams had the same winning percentage, then the conclusion that one was better (different) than the other would be weakened by this similarity.

As another example of a difference comparison, examine the argument: "The federal budget deficit increased from $800 billion three years ago to $912 billion this year. We've got to do something about it before it destroys our economy." What if the federal budget deficit were 4% of the Gross National

Product (the measure of goods and services produced in a year) three years ago and 4% this year also? Here, a similarity found between the deficits of the two years being compared weakens the conclusion that the federal budget deficit is getting worse. Thus, differences weaken arguments comparing similarities, and similarities weaken arguments comparing differences.

IDENTIFYING COMPARISON REASONING

Cue words can help identify comparisons. Watch for such comparative terms as "like," "similar to," "same as," "greater (or less) than," "better (or worse) than," and "increased (or decreased)." Some comparisons, however, are implied rather than stated. For example, someone might say, "Oh, I wouldn't travel by plane. It's too dangerous." You might ask "dangerous compared to what?" If a higher percentage of people are injured or killed using alternate methods of travel (automobiles, trains), then the statement is weakened considerably.

> In examining comparisons, ask yourself,
> * How are the cases similar; how are they different?

EVALUATING COMPARISON REASONING

This skill involves *evaluating comparison arguments*. It is not the same activity as "compare and contrast," where you are asked to find the similarities and differences between two items; i.e., "Compare and contrast the American and French Revolutions." In evaluating comparison arguments you, on your own, are to recognize that a comparison argument is being made and, without being told, ask about the similarities and differences of the two cases being compared.

Reasoning by Generalization

This kind of reasoning includes both definitional and statistical generalizations. The generalization, "No U.S. senator is under 30 years of age" is an example of a *definitional generalization*, since by legal definition, a United States senator must be at least 30 years of age.

Statistical generalization is important to evaluating historical arguments. Statistical generalizations argue that what is true for some (part or sample) of a group (such as wars, women, or songs) will be true in roughly the same way for all of the group. For example, Maribeth might argue that since the bite of pizza she took (sample) is cold, the whole pizza (the whole group) is cold.

Statistical generalizations can be further subdivided into two types. *Hard generalizations* are those applied to all (or none) of the members of a group, e.g., the whole cold pizza above, or a statement like "All the apples have fallen off the tree." A hard generalization is disproved by one counterexample (contrary case). For example, if there is one apple still on the tree, the generalization is disproved.

Soft generalizations are those applied to most (or few) members of a group, e.g., "Most people remember the Vietnam War." A soft generalization is not disproved by one—or even several—contrary cases, but the generalization is weakened as the contrary cases add up. For example, if someone says that Luis does not remember the Vietnam War, the generalization is not disproved. If, however, that person cites fifty people who do not remember the Vietnam War, the generalization is getting shaky.

The probability that a statistical generalization is correct increases with the size of the sample and the degree to which a sample is representative of the whole group. Your generalization that "Nella is prompt" is more likely to be accurate if she was on time on all twenty occasions when she was supposed to meet you than if she was on time the only time she was supposed to meet you.

Representativeness is even more important than size in generalizations. In the pizza example the sample is quite small (only one bite from the whole pizza) but very representative—if one part of the pizza is cold, it is highly likely that the whole pizza is cold. Similarly, presidential election polls are small (about 1200 people polled) but usually very accurate, since those sampled are quite representative of the whole electorate. If you think of the whole group of voters as a circle, a presidential election poll might look like Figure 1.

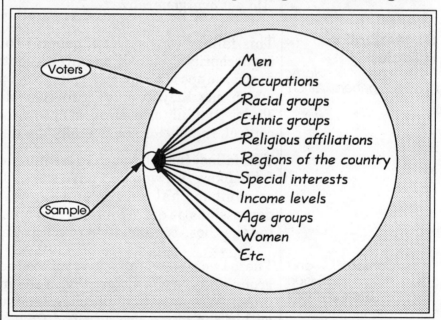

Voters

Sample

Men
Occupations
Racial groups
Ethnic groups
Religious affiliations
Regions of the country
Special interests
Income levels
Age groups
Women
Etc.

Figure 1. The sample should represent all these groups of voters (and many more) in the same proportion as they make up the whole electorate.

**IDENTIFYING
GENERALIZATIONS**

You can recognize statistical generalizations by watching for their cue words ("all," "none," "some," "most," "a majority," "few") or plural nouns ("women," "farmers," or "people").

EVALUATING
GENERALIZATIONS

Questions you should ask when evaluating generalizations include the following.

> • How large is the sample?
> The strength of a statistical generalization is improved by larger sized sampling.
> • How representative is the sample?
> If you picture the generalization as a little circle and a big circle, as in Figure 1, the question becomes: Does the little circle have all the same subgroups in the same proportion as the big circle?

You should not, however, be concerned only with evaluating generalizations that other people make. You should also be concerned with how far you can legitimately generalize from what you know.

For example, if you learned that slaves on ten large cotton plantations in Maryland in the 1850s were brutally treated, you might generalize that slaves on most large cotton plantations in Maryland at that time were brutally treated. You would be on much shakier ground, however, to generalize that slaves on most plantations were brutally treated at all times. You really have no information about slaves on, say, small Virginia tobacco plantations in the 1720s, so you shouldn't make such a broad generalization. The warning is, "Do not overgeneralize."

Generalization Fallacies
Hasty generalization

This fallacy consists of a general conclusion based on an inappropriately small or unrepresentative sample. For example, suppose a reporter polls three people in Illinois, all of whom say they support gun control. If the reporter concludes that all (or even most) people in Illinois support gun control, then he or she is making a hasty generalization.

This fallacy includes such oversimplifications as "If it weren't for bankers, we wouldn't have wars." To avoid such fallacies, remember that any group (such as people, wars, or depressions) is quite complex and must be carefully sampled to take those complexities into account.

Composition and division (stereotyping)

These two related fallacies confuse the characteristics of the group and the characteristics of the individuals within that group. In composition, the characteristics of the individual(s) within the group are ascribed (given) to the whole group. ("She's a good lawyer, so the law firm she is a member of must be a good firm.") In division, characteristics that belong to the group as a whole are assumed to belong to each of the individuals. ("She's a member of a good law firm, so she must be a good lawyer.")

These fallacies are commonly referred to as *stereotyping*, which is defined as "applying preconceived ideas to a group or members of a group." This results in the groups or individuals being judged before we really know them. This act of prejudging is where we derive the word *prejudice*. "You're Jewish, so you must be well educated" and "Of course he's a drinker, he's Irish!" are examples of stereotype statements.

Special pleading

In this fallacy the arguer presents a conclusion based on information favorable to the argument while ignoring unfavorable information. ("Mom, I should be able to go to the dance. I passed my history test and got an 'A' in math." [...omitting the information that I failed science and English.]) A good argument avoids this fallacy by including unfavorable information and overcoming it with compelling reasons for accepting the thesis or conclusion.

Reasoning by Proof (evidence, example, or authority)

These types of reasoning concern whether or not the evidence or authority used supports the point being argued. It does not concern the strengths and weakness of the evidence itself (see the **Evidence** section of the Guide). Similarly, the word "proof" as used here does not mean absolute proof—as in mathematics—but rather refers to methods used to support an argument or interpretation.

This is generally a legitimate method of supporting an argument. For example, a doctor might be called to testify in court to support the argument that a claimant had certain injuries (proof by authority). A biologist might explain the results of several investigations (example), cite evidence gathered (evidence), and quote the written opinions of several experts (authority) to support an argument on the effects of toxic waste.

IDENTIFYING PROOF
REASONING

Proof reasoning can be identified by cue words such as "for example," "for instance," "according to," "authority," and "expert." When evaluating argument by proof, you should look at the answers to several questions:

EVALUATING PROOF

Evidence

Examples

Authority

- Does the evidence prove the point being argued? Does it support the point under consideration?
- Are the examples pertinent to the argument?
- Is this person an expert on this particular topic? What are the qualifications of the authority? Are they presented?
- Do other authorities agree with these conclusions? Are there any authorities who disagree with the conclusion? Are counterarguments acknowledged and/or refuted?

**Fallacies
of Proof**

*Irrelevant
proof*

Arguments which present compelling evidence that does not apply to the argument in question are fallacies of irrelevant proof. For example, "If you flunk me, I'll lose my scholarship" and "Everyone else does it" are fallacies of irrelevant proof. As a further example, suppose Senator Smith is accused of taking bribes to vote for certain laws and, in his defense, presents a great deal of evidence that shows he is a good family man. This evidence does not concern his actions as a senator and is thus irrelevant to the charges. Good arguments avoid this fallacy by sticking to the issue under question.

*Negative
proof*

This fallacy type presents a conclusion based on the lack or absence of evidence to the contrary. For example, "There is no evidence that Senator Macklem is an honest woman, so it's obvious she is a crook" or "Since you haven't proven that there is no Santa Claus, there must be one." Remember that you must present evidence to **support** your conclusions when you are making a case.

*Prevalent
proof*

Related to the fallacy of negative proof, this fallacy concludes that something must be the case because "everyone knows" it is the case. Such arguments as "Everyone knows she's a winner" and "Politicians can't be trusted; everyone knows that" are examples of the prevalent proof fallacy. Remember, in previous times "everyone knew" that the sun revolved around the earth! The critical thinker sometimes asks questions even about things which everyone knows.

Numbers

A conclusion that the argument is right solely because of the great amount of evidence gathered commits the fallacy of numbers. For example, "We checked hundreds of thousands of government records, so our theory must be right."

Notice that no mention is made of what the "government records" contained—the argument only states that they were "checked." A great deal of evidence can be amassed to support a slanted perspective or an argument using poor reasoning or faulty assumptions. When constructing arguments, check them not only for strong evidence but also for sound reasoning and assumptions.

*Appeal
to authority*

A conclusion that is based only on the statement of an expert commits the appeal-to-authority fallacy. Such arguments conclude, "I'm right because I'm an expert" and lack additional supporting evidence. For example, the argument "It must be true because it says so right here in the book" is based only on the "authority" of the book's author. Arguments must be judged on the strength of their evidence and their reasoning rather than solely on the authority of their authors.

*Appeal to the
golden mean*

This logical fallacy is committed when the argument is made that the conclusion is right because it is moderate (between the extreme views). If someone argued, "Some people say Adolf Hitler was right in what he did, while others say he was one of the most evil leaders in history. These views are so extreme that a more moderate view must be right. He must have been an average leader," he or she would be appealing to the golden mean. (Of course, the "extreme" view that Hitler was evil is right in this case.)

This fallacy can be avoided by realizing that there is no reason for an extreme view to be wrong simply because it is extreme. At one time it was considered "extreme" to think that women should vote or that people would fly.

Reasoning by Debate (eliminating alternatives)

Reasoning by debate helps a person see why one interpretation should be believed over other interpretations and puts an interpretation into a context. It is not surprising, therefore, that articles in historical journals frequently begin by a survey of other interpretations of the topic under study and an attempt to refute opposing interpretations.

This type of reasoning advances an argument by referring to and attempting to show the weaknesses of alternative interpretations. This attempt to disprove, called debating, is not only acceptable, but desirable. For example, someone might argue, "Peter thinks Mi-Ling will get the lead role in the play, but he's wrong. Lucetta has a better voice and more acting experience, so she'll get the lead." A historian might argue, "Although the traditional view is that slavery is the main cause of the Civil War, people who hold that view are wrong. Economic problems, especially over the tariff, were the main cause of the bloody war." Both are applying reasoning by debate.

IDENTIFYING DEBATES

Cue words for this type of reasoning include "other people believe," "the traditional view is," "other views are wrong because," "older interpretations," and "other viewpoints are."

EVALUATING DEBATES

To help evaluate debate reasoning, ask questions like the following.

> - Have all reasonable alternatives been considered? Have they all been eliminated as possibilities?
> - Does this author attack the other views in a fair way?
> - What might the authors of the other views say in response to this argument?

In eliminating possible alternatives, the author must be careful to attack the argument rather than the arguer, to present reasoned evidence against the argument, and to fairly interpret the alternative argument under consideration. This form of questioning can also be helpful when there is a lack of information.

Fallacies of Debate *Either-or*

This fallacy presents a conclusion that since A and B were the only possible explanations—and since A was not possible, B is proven to be the explanation. For example, "Only Willis and Cross were around, but Willis was swimming so Cross must have done it." What if someone else was actually around but no one saw him or her?

Of course, eliminating alternatives can be very important to reasoning a problem through, as Sherlock Holmes demonstrates so well. But one must be careful to ask: Have all alternatives been eliminated? Could it be both alternatives? Don't let yourself be "boxed in" by this type of reasoning.

Attacking the arguer

(In logical terminology, this is called *ad hominem*—Latin for "to the man.") This fallacy occurs when statements are directed at the person making the argument rather than at the arguments presented. For example, the statement "No one should listen to what Mrs. Rouge says. She's a Communist" is an attack on Mrs. Rouge personally rather than on the statement she made.

Sometimes the attack is more subtle, such as a look of disgust, a negative comment ("I don't believe you just said that"), or sarcastic laughter. Good arguments avoid this fallacy by refuting the argument, not the person.

Straw man

This is the technique of attacking the opponents' argument by adding to or changing what a person said, then attacking the additions or changes. For example, Johannas says he's opposed to capital punishment, and Thibedeau replies, "People like you who oppose punishing criminals make me sick." (Johannas did not say he opposed punishing criminals.) When constructing an argument, remember to be fair and argue against what your opponents said, not your version of what they said.

There are many methods of trying to prove something. The types of reasoning explained above (cause and effect; comparisons; generalizations; proof by evidence, example, or authority; and debate) are all methods of proof to be considered when evaluating historical arguments. The next section examines assumptions, which are like reasoning in that they lead to conclusions (assertions). They are different from reasoning, however, in that they are not always consciously argued. Authors frequently do not realize the assumptions they are making.

Assumptions

GENERAL UNSTATED ASSUMPTIONS

SPECIFIC UNSTATED ASSUMPTIONS

An assumption is the part of an argument containing the ideas or opinions that the arguer takes for granted. Stated assumptions are not of concern for the purposes of this Guide. When authors say they are assuming something, all you decide is whether you agree with the stated assumption.

Unstated assumptions are more difficult to recognize. There are two types of unstated assumptions: the general, more encompassing type and the specific type.

These assumptions are part of the argument as a whole and, as such, cannot be identified by rewriting particular arguments. In any argument there are an infinite number of such assumptions. For example, if you say you are going to the store to buy a TV, you are making the general assumptions that the store will be there, that you won't die on the way, that they'll have televisions in stock, and so forth. Some assumptions are trivial or unlikely, but others are very important. For example, if the President of the United States says, "We will not agree to the Soviet proposal to have both countries eliminate half of their missiles because we cannot check on them adequately," he is assuming the Soviets cannot be trusted. If, on the other hand, the President agreed to missile reductions without a means of verifying Soviet reductions, he would then be assuming the Soviets can be trusted. He might or might not be right in either case. The important point is that we should recognize his assumption.

General assumptions shape historical interpretations. A historian who assumes that economics drives people's behavior will select economic information and write from that perspective; a historian who assumes that politics, in the form of power and compromise, shapes society will focus on that area in both research and writing.

To understand specific unstated assumptions you need to know something about the form of arguments. As was explained in the section on **Assertions**, arguments are made up of the conclusion and the rest of the argument, which is designed to prove the conclusion. The sentences that comprise the rest of the argument are called *premises*.

Short arguments take the form of *premise, premise, conclusion*. A well-known example is: "Socrates is a man. All men are mortal. Therefore, Socrates is mortal." In premise, premise, conclusion format, this would be:

Premise: Socrates is a man.
Premise: All men are mortal.
Conclusion: Therefore, Socrates is mortal.

If the above argument "looks funny," it's because people rarely talk this way. In normal speech, we often state the conclusion first: "I should be able to go outside now. My homework is done." It is also common to not state one of the premises or the conclusion at all. For example, if we are trying to decide who should pay for the broken vase, you might say, "Well, Joaquin pushed me into it." Your point (although you did not state it) is that Joaquin should pay.

When you leave out a premise, you are making an assumption. For example, the argument "We should spend our vacation in the mountains because we need a rest," can be rewritten this way:

Premise: We need a rest.

Premise: ??

Conclusion: (Therefore) we should spend our vacation in the mountains.

The missing premise is the assumption.

IDENTIFYING ASSUMPTIONS

You can figure out what the assumption is by asking, "What has to be true for this conclusion to be true?" In the above case, the missing premise (assumption) is: "The mountains are a good place to rest."

EVALUATING ASSUMPTIONS

When you have identified an assumption, evaluate it by asking if the assumption is correct. Assumptions are frequently related to the beliefs and values of the author, as explained in the next section.

Values

Values are conditions that the person making an argument believes are important, worthwhile, or intrinsically good for themselves, their family, their country, and their world. Money, success, friendship, love, health, peace, power, freedom, and equality are examples of things people may value.

It is often important to discover the underlying values of the author of an argument, since assumptions made by an author are often related to the author's beliefs and values. This will help you understand why the viewpoint is argued the way it is, and, in cases where your values may be different from the author's values, it will help you understand why you might disagree with the argument. For example, if you believe that peace is more important than demonstrating power, then you are going to disagree with an argument which says that since Country A increased its power by attacking Country B; it was right to attack.

IDENTIFYING VALUE STATEMENTS

Clues to an author's value judgments are found in sentences containing words such as "good," "bad," "right," "wrong," "justified," "should," or "should not." For example, if someone says "The United States was wrong (value judgment) to drop the atomic bomb on Hiroshima because so many people were killed," that person is saying that life (value) is more important than the other conditions or values involved (power, peace vs. war, etc.).

To help identify an author's values, ask:
- Who wrote this?
- What beliefs does this person hold?

When you have identified a value judgment in an argument, you can then examine it. For example, consider the argument, "We should have capital punishment because criminals will commit fewer crimes if they think they might be executed."

EVALUATING VALUE
STATEMENTS

---

1. *Separate the argument into its factual and value parts.*

   Factual part:

   Capital punishment will make criminals commit fewer crimes. (Notice that this could be investigated by examining statistics on the number of crimes with and without capital punishment.)

   Value assumption:

   Fewer crimes is good (a desirable outcome).

2. *Rephrase the value statement into general terms.*

   Anything (general term) which causes fewer crimes is good (value judgment).

3. *Ask yourself if the value statement is right in all instances.*

   Is the statement, "Anything which causes fewer crimes is good" true? Can you think of cases in which you might not agree? Substitute some specific situations and see if the statement is still right. For example, "Jailing all people accused of a crime, whether found guilty or not, would also cause fewer crimes to be committed. Should we do this?"

This kind of questioning will help both you and the person who originally made the claim think more fully about the value(s) behind the claim.

Three general questions can be used to test the worthiness of value claims.
- Are you willing to use this value in all situations?
- What would society be like if everyone believed and acted on this value?
- Would you want the value applied to you?

The next page contains two charts you may find helpful for reminding you of methods you can use to analyze the viewpoints presented in this book. As you proceed, refer to this "Guide to Critical Thinking" to help you with the lessons.

A MODEL FOR ANALYZING ARGUMENTS

A model is a way of organizing information. One type of model is an acronym where each letter in the model stands for a word. The model outlined here is **ARMEAR**. Each letter will remind you of a part of arguments to examine.

A	Author	• Who wrote this interpretation and why? • What are the author's values or beliefs? • What can you learn about the author?
R	Relevant Information	• What do you know about the topic being argued or topics related to it?
M	Main Point	• What is the main point or thesis of the argument?
E	Evidence	• What evidence is presented to support the argument? • How reliable is it? • What are the sources of the evidence?
A	Assumptions	• What assumptions does the author make?
R	Reasoning	• What reasoning is used in the argument? Cause and effect? Comparison? Generalization? Proof? Debate? • How strong is the reasoning?

FIVE MAIN PARTS OF AN ARGUMENT

Assertion, main point, or thesis	• What is the author trying to prove?
Evidence	• Is the source given for information? • How strong is it? Primary? Reason to distort? Other evidence to verify? Public or private? (**PROP**).
Reasoning	• Cause and Effect — Is the connection shown? Are there other possible causes? Is there an important cause previous to the one proposed? • Comparisons — How are the two cases different and how are they similar? • Generalizations — How large and representative is the sample? • Proof — Does the evidence support the point being made? How many examples are given? Is this authority an expert on this topic? • Debate — Does the author attack other views in a fair way? Have all possible alternatives been eliminated?
Assumptions	• What must be true if the thesis is true (acceptable)?
Values	• Do I agree with these values? • Is this value position right in all instances?

LESSON 1   Identifying Sources

When someone makes a claim or states an opinion, we should require that person to give information (often examples), and tell us the source of the information. The source is the person, written document, or object from which the information came. The source may also be the person making the claim, based on his or her observations or experiences.

When evaluating claims or opinions you should ask the person:

- What information do you have to support your claims?
- From what source do you get the information?

Q Label each item below with the appropriate letter.

S A **source** of information is given.

N **No** source of information is given.

_____1. A 1986 CBS-New York poll found that 51% of those surveyed thought the federal government created more problems than it solved. This was down from 63% in 1981.

_____2. Since 1960 the birth rate among blacks has declined tremendously. The effect is that ghetto areas are getting smaller in many parts of the country.

_____3. A Union lieutenant in North Carolina said in 1865 that Southern whites would not accept former slaves as free men.

_____4. Many Southern veterans of the Civil War came home in 1865 to scenes of destruction.

_____5. After the Civil War, Southern states held down blacks by passing "Black Codes" which limited the rights of ex-slaves. Blacks were not allowed to testify against whites in court. They could not marry out of their race, nor could they move freely about the countryside.

_____6. Most teenagers like rock music. Of course there are exceptions—some teenagers even like classical music best.

_____7. After the 1866 elections, Congress passed the Military Reconstruction Act which divided the South into five military districts, each ruled by a Northern general.

_____8. The Republicans in the South Carolina State House in the 1860s and 1870s spent a great deal of time in the refreshment room, eating and drinking excessively at taxpayer's expense.[1]

[1] *Report on Public Frauds* (1877), p. 170, statement by Lewis Grant, a porter (a person who carries things and waits on people) in the South Carolina State House.

LESSON 2   Evaluating Sources

Primary Sources

A primary source is evidence given (often written down) by a person who was present at, or part of, the event reported on. Or, it is an object that was **part of the event.**

To determine the type of source, ask yourself:

- Was the person or object present at the time of the event?
- Did the person see the event on which s/he is reporting?

If so, the source is a primary source.

Q Label each item below with the appropriate letter.

P   It is a **primary** source.

S   It is a **secondary** source.

_____1.   Phillip said he saw Lorelei at the dance.

_____2.   Historian Daniel Boorstin stated in his book, *A History of the United States*, (1981), that Thaddeus Stevens, a Radical Republican in the House of Representatives, was a vengeful person.

_____3.   An article in a Northern newspaper stated that corruption was not widespread in Southern reconstruction legislatures.

_____4.   President Lincoln said he favored a policy of "malice toward none" in dealing with the Southern states.

_____5.   A photograph taken in 1866 shows a husband and wife sitting outside their shack.

Reason to Lie

People have a reason to lie when they make themselves or their group look good or when they help their own interests (for example, when they make more money). People

[Continued on next page.]

[Continued from previous page.]

generally have no reason to lie when they (often without realizing it) make themselves look bad or their enemy look good.

Q Label each item below with the appropriate letter.

    R The person has a **reason** to lie.

    N The person has **no** reason to lie.

_____6. Jean admitted that she was the one who broke the leg of the table.

_____7. A Democratic politician in Louisiana who was defeated for governor by a Republican said the Republicans were corrupt.

_____8. A black leader in the South Carolina Legislature said he took a $5,000 bribe.

_____9. Historian Winthrop Jordan said in a book published in 1957 that Black Codes were passed after the Civil War to control blacks.

_____10. A drawing done in May 1866 showed freed men voting in an orderly way. Several blacks are smiling.

Corroboration

Corroboration means finding other evidence to support evidence you already have. If I claim that Bill was a great baseball player and you find a newspaper article saying that Bill was a great baseball player, you have corroborated what I said. What evidence would you search for to corroborate the evidence in the following?

11. Question #2 (p. 20)

12. Question #7 (above)

LESSON 3   Evaluating Evidence about Reconstruction

Evaluate the following pieces of evidence by listing strengths and weaknesses of each. If you need help, refer to the section on **evidence** in the "Guide to Critical Thinking," Unit 1.

1. Jose tells his father that the teacher kept him after school unfairly. He says another student was talking, but since the teacher doesn't like Jose, she assumed it was him talking.

    STRENGTHS   WEAKNESSES

2. *Star*, a weekly newspaper of strange stories, recently ran an article asserting that UFO bases were found in New Mexico.

    STRENGTHS   WEAKNESSES

3. W. Beverly Nash, a black Senator in South Carolina, stated in 1872 that Senator Leslie gave him a package containing $5000 to vote in favor of certain bills. He said he already favored the bills, so the money didn't influence his vote. He said he kept the money because he might as well have it and invest it.

    STRENGTHS   WEAKNESSES

[Continued on next page.]

[Continued from previous page.]

4. Governor Chamberlain stated to two Charleston, South Carolina, newspapers in 1875 that until he took over as governor fraud (dishonesty) was everywhere in the government. Legislative expenses alone amounted to over $2 million. It was stealing pure and simple. Chamberlain was running for reelection in 1875 against Radical Republicans. He said the only way to save South Carolina was to reelect him.

    STRENGTHS   WEAKNESSES

5. Historian Bernard A. Weisberger in his book *The Impact of Our Past,* published in 1972, says that hundreds of blacks sat in state legislatures in the South from 1867 to 1872 but were a majority only in the lower houses of South Carolina and Mississippi, and then just for a short while.

    STRENGTHS   WEAKNESSES

LESSON 4   Recognizing and Assessing Cause-and-Effect Reasoning

Recognizing Cause-and-Effect Reasoning

In order to be cause-and-effect reasoning the statement has to argue that something caused, led to, or brought about something else.

Q Label each item below.

> **C**   Item uses **cause-and-effect** reasoning.
>
> **N**   Item does **not** use cause-and-effect reasoning.

_____1.   I missed the bus so I was late for school.

_____2.   I really enjoyed watching *Tom Sawyer* on television Tuesday night.

_____3.   Our administration got the Soviets to negotiate arms reduction by increasing and strengthening our military defenses.

_____4.   When President Lincoln was assassinated, the chance for compromise and a successful reconstruction of the South was ended.

_____5.   President Andrew Johnson was not the leader Abraham Lincoln was.

Evaluating Cause-and-Effect Reasoning

Q Evaluate the following cause-and-effect arguments. Refer to the section on **cause-and-effect** reasoning in the "Guide to Critical Thinking," Unit 1, if you need help. Note especially the questions for evaluating cause and effect. Make a diagram of each argument, if necessary.

6. What has led to our drug problem? The decline in our values. We started values-free education. We have to teach values in school.

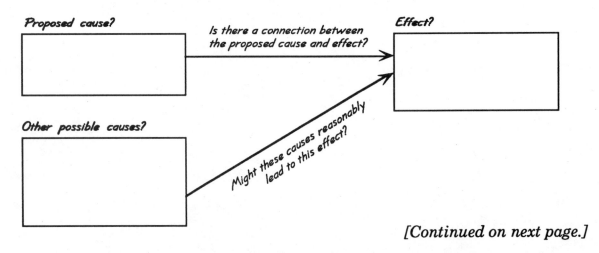

Proposed cause?

Is there a connection between the proposed cause and effect?

Effect?

Other possible causes?

Might these causes reasonably lead to this effect?

[Continued on next page.]

[Continued from previous page.]

7. The problem of homeless people is a result of the government cuts in money to public housing in the 1980s. Since 1980 the number of homeless has risen dramatically to 2.5–3 million people.

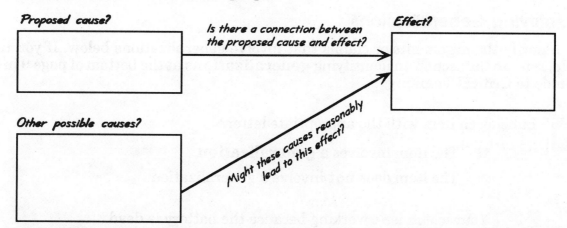

8. The Military Reconstruction Act used troops to ensure black voting. Naturally, Southern whites resented this, which resulted in the racism of the Ku Klux Klan and the Jim Crow laws.

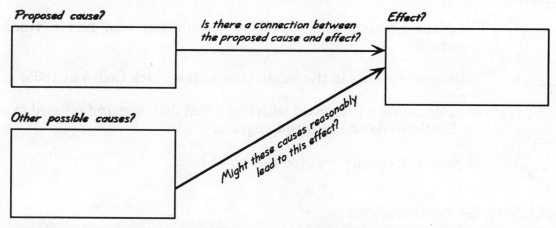

9. Andrew Johnson campaigned against the Radical Republicans in the congressional elections of 1866. Many voters, however, felt Johnson had no business doing that, so the Republicans ended up winning most of the congressional elections.

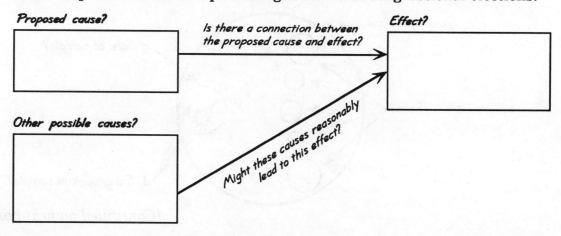

LESSON 5   Identifying and Evaluating Generalizations

Identifying Generalizations

Identify the arguments or claims that involve generalizations below. If you need help, refer to the section on identifying **generalizations** at the bottom of page 9 in the "Guide to Critical Thinking."

Q   Label each item with the appropriate letter.

    G   The item involves a **generalization**.

    N   The item does **not** involve a generalization.

_____1.   Your watch isn't working because the battery is dead.

_____2.   People who jog tend to keep their cholesterol low.

_____3.   President Lincoln favored the 10% Plan.

_____4.   Thaddeus Stevens was a Radical Republican who had a vindictive personality.

_____5.   State governments in the South passed the Black Codes in 1865.

_____6.   The Republicans disagreed with President Johnson and refused to allow the Southern delegates into Congress.

_____7.   Almost all freedmen wanted their own land.

Evaluating Generalizations

Evaluate the following generalizations. If you need help, see pages 9 and 10 on evaluating **generalizations** in the "Guide to Critical Thinking" (Unit 1). Use the figure (below) to help you visualize the generalization for each item.

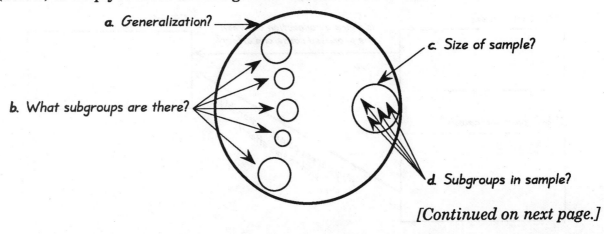

a. Generalization?

c. Size of sample?

b. What subgroups are there?

d. Subgroups in sample?

[Continued on next page.]

[Continued from previous page.]

8. Most voters apparently disagreed with President Johnson in the election of 1866. Johnson asked people to vote for Conservatives, but the voters elected a great majority of Moderate and Radical Republicans.

    a. What is the generalization?

    b. What subgroups make up the large group (the voters)?

    c. How large is the sample?

    d. Does the sample have all the same subgroups? (Is it representative?)

    e. How strong is the generalization?

9. Carpetbaggers were Northerners who came to the South after the Civil War for political power and financial gain.

    a. What is the generalization?

    b. What subgroups make up the large group?

    c. How large is the sample?

    d. Does the sample have all the same subgroups? (Is it representative?)

    e. How strong is the generalization?

[Continued on next page.]

[Continued from previous page.]

10. While most Southerners did not belong to the Ku Klux Klan, they allowed it to commit acts of violence against blacks for more than a decade without trying to stop it.

    How strong is this generalization?

LESSON 6   How Corrupt Were Reconstruction Governments?

After the Civil War the country had to decide on terms for bringing the Southern states back into the Union. President Johnson allowed them back into the Union on generous terms. But Republicans, especially Radical Republicans, disagreed with the President. In the Reconstruction Act of 1867, they voted to send United States soldiers to the South to make sure blacks could vote. Soon Republican whites and blacks controlled the Southern governments. In this lesson, two historians take opposing positions on how corrupt these Republican governments were.

Historian A

(1) Northern "carpetbaggers," working with Southern "scalawags," came to the South after the Civil War to take advantage of the unfortunate situation there. Carpetbaggers wanted to make money and seize political power for the Republican Party. Scalawags wanted power and money for themselves.

(2) Under the Radical governments of the carpetbaggers and scalawags, blacks could vote, but many wealthy whites (plantation owners) could not. As a result, elections in the South were a farce. Thousands of ignorant, irresponsible blacks, directed by their white bosses, voted without knowing even the names of the men for whom they were voting.[1]

(3) The Northern Radicals were lying when they said they wanted Negroes to vote and hold office in the name of justice. This is shown when one notices that few of the Northern states allowed the Negroes to vote and none ever promoted a Negro into any office.

(4) The South was now plunged by this misgovernment into corruption and plundering beyond belief. Radical Republican Legislatures, supported by military power, piled up expenses against their poor states to fantastic heights. In Florida the cost of printing in 1869 was more than the entire cost of the state government in 1860. In Arkansas a Negro was given $9,000 for repairing a bridge which had originally cost $500. In South Carolina the legislature voted extra pay of $1,000 to the Speaker for his efficient service when he lost $1,000 on a horse race.

(5) A Congressional Committee reported that one of the leading carpetbag (Republican) governors made over $100,000 during his first year in office though his salary was $8,000.[2] Another carpetbag governor was charged with stealing and selling the food of the Freedmen's Bureau which was intended for the relief of helpless and ragged ex-slaves. F.J. Moses, scalawag, stated that he received $15,000 while governor of South Carolina for approving a large printing bill.[3]

(6) Naturally, decent white men in the South detested this misgovernment. Resentment on the part of whites led to violence by the Ku Klux Klan and others. The Radical Republicans in Congress had run the South at gunpoint which gave them political power for a time, but when that time ran out, blacks and whites were hostile toward each other. Republican rule needlessly crippled the political and economic systems of the South and set back the rights of blacks for generations.

[Continued on next page.]

[Continued from previous page.]

Endnotes for Historian A

[1] W.L. Fleming, *Documentary History of Reconstruction.* (Cleveland, OH, 1906–1907), Vol. II, p. 44 Statement of Samuel Hale, a Unionist (a Southerner who supported the North during the Civil War), in 1867 to a Congressional Committee:

"I wish you could have seen the poor, ignorant blacks giving their 'bits of paper,' as they called their printed ballots, when they knew no more of the names on them...than you did."

[2] Ibid., Vol. II, p. 39 Report of Mr. Speer and Mr. Archer of the Congressional Investigating Committee in 1872. House Report No. 92, 42 Congress, 2nd Session, p. 24.

[3] Ibid., Vol. II, p. 41 Statement by F.J. Moses in 1873, contained in Report on Public Frauds in South Carolina, p. 317.

Historian B

(1) After the Civil War, Republicans in Congress voted to send troops into the South to protect the rights of blacks freed from slavery by the Emancipation Proclamation and the Thirteenth Amendment. Southern state governments were now controlled by three groups of Republicans — carpetbaggers, scalawags, and freedmen. These Republican governments have been attacked for being corrupt, but these criticisms are unfair. Actually, the Reconstruction governments were no more corrupt than other governments at the time, and they accomplished many worthwhile reforms.

(2) Among the Northern carpetbaggers who moved to the South were, to be sure, some who were interested in power and profit. Most were in ordinary occupations, however, such as teachers and missionaries, who were sincerely interested in helping the freedmen. Scalawags have likewise been stereotyped as traitors looking for political power. But scalawags were simply Southern whites who didn't like government in the South under the Democrats. Quite naturally they turned to the other political party to bring about change.

(3) The new Republican state governments wrote very good state constitutions which contained a number of important reforms, such as free public education. On the other hand, there was definitely some corruption in the governments. But the corruption has to be set in its proper context.

(4) First, much of the increased spending was for construction, especially railroad construction, and most of the profits from the corruption involved in railroads did not go to the Republicans. The people who profited most from the bribes were the Southern construction contractors, business investors, and railroad promoters. Most of the debt increases in Southern states resulted from grants and guarantees to railroad promoters, among whom were always some native white Democrats.[1] In Florida, more than 60% of the debt was from railroad bonds. Most of Alabama's reconstruction debt—$18,000,000 out of $20,500,000—was from state bonds for money to assist railroads.

(5) White Democrats in several states greatly exaggerated the actual increase in the size of the state debts. In Mississippi the Democrats claimed the Radicals had added $20,000,000 to the state debt, when it was, in fact, only $500,000. The claim by Democrats of the debt increase for Alabama was $30,000,000 when it was only $2,500,000. In most other states, when loans to the railroads were subtracted, the increases in state debts for which Radicals were responsible appear far smaller. Actually,

[Continued on next page.]

Historian B

[Continued from previous page.]

a good deal of white planter protest against alleged corruption in the Radical government was really against Radical tax policies which made them pay their fair share (they had paid very low taxes before the Civil War) and pay it for services (such as education) to Negroes.

(6) As a matter of fact, taxes, government spending, and public debts were bound to increase in the Southern states after the war no matter who controlled the state governments. For there was no way to escape the cost of physical reconstruction—such as repair of buildings and bridges. And much of this physical reconstruction took place while Radicals were in office. They expanded the state railroad systems, increased public services, and provided public school systems—in some states for the first time. Since schools and other public services were now provided for Negroes as well as for whites, a considerable increase in the cost of state government could hardly have been avoided. In Florida, between 1869 and 1873, the number of children in public schools tripled, while in South Carolina the number quadrupled.

(7) The period after the Civil War was a time of great corruption in government, as shown in the incredible swindling by the Tweed Ring in New York City. Further, the state governments in the South after the Democrats took control again in the 1870s often turned out to be just as corrupt as the Republican governments they had criticized. One Democratic state treasurer embezzled $316,000 and eight other state treasurers were convicted of embezzlement.

(8) The corruption of the Republicans was not unusual; their spending was certainly reasonable given the circumstances; and the corruption was not limited to them alone. The white Southerners who were so critical were often hypocrites who were involved in corruption themselves. The Reconstruction governments accomplished a great deal under difficult circumstances. It is time to stop exaggerating the faults of the Reconstruction governments and look at the record fairly.

Endnotes for Historian B

[1] Ellan Lonn (a historian), *Reconstruction in Louisiana After 1868*. (New York, 1918), pp. 36–37:

"Such measures [railroad bond issues] were supported by members of both parties, often introduced by Democrats, in every case supported by a large majority of Democrats in both houses."

 Historian A

1. What is the main idea of Historian A's argument?

[Continued on next page.]

[Continued from previous page.]

2. What assumption does Historian A make in the following?

  a. Paragraph 3

  b. Paragraph 5, first sentence

3. Find one piece of evidence and evaluate it.

4. Evaluate the reasoning in the following.

  a. Paragraph 1

  b. Paragraphs 4 and 5

  c. Paragraph 6

5. Which words in the first sentence of Paragraph 4 make a value judgment?

_____6. What does Historian A seem to feel largely determined the history of Reconstruction?

  A. Laws and politics

  B. Economics

  C. The development of new machines and tools

  D. Individual people and what they do

  E. Groups of people and their beliefs

[Continued on next page.]

[Continued from previous page.]

 Historian B

7. What is the main idea of Historian B's argument?

8. What assumption does Historian B make in Paragraph 6, first and second sentences?

9. Find one piece of evidence and evaluate it.

10. Evaluate the reasoning in the following.
    a. Paragraph 2, first and second sentences

    b. Paragraph 5, last sentence

11. Which words in the first sentence of Paragraph 3 make a value judgment?

_____12. What does Historian B seem to feel largely determined the history of Reconstruction?
    A. Laws and politics
    B. Economics
    C. The development of new machines and tools
    D. Individual people and what they do
    E. Groups of people and their beliefs

LESSON 7   To What Extent Was Reconstruction a Tragic Era?

After the Civil War the country faced the challenge of bringing the 11 seceded states back into the Union. This period from 1865 to 1877 is called the Reconstruction era. During the first phase of Reconstruction, in 1865, Presidents Lincoln and Johnson allowed Southern whites to form governments on generous terms. In the second phase, the Radical Republicans in Congress took control of Reconstruction and imposed more restrictions on the Southern states. The issue of protecting the rights of freedmen, former slaves who had been freed by the Emancipation Proclamation and the 13th Amendment, was a central dispute at this time.

The third phase of Reconstruction began gradually as the Southern whites regained control of their state governments in the 1870s.

In this lesson, three viewpoints deal primarily with the question of the rights of blacks and whether Reconstruction governments in the Southern states, controlled by the Republican party, were a good idea. The viewpoints deal with the issue of whether Reconstruction should be called a tragic era, and if so, why. It will not deal with the constitutional question of which branch of government, Congress or the President, should have controlled Reconstruction, and it will not deal with the impeachment trial of Andrew Johnson.

The first viewpoint actually is derived from two historians who represent what has been called the "Dunning School" on Reconstruction. The second viewpoint represents the "revisionist school"—an effort to revise the original Dunning interpretation. The third viewpoint is a more modern interpretation which has no "school" label. In some of the earlier interpretations the word Negro is used for blacks—the word has been retained in these summaries of the viewpoints. So "Negro" and "black" are both used in the viewpoints.

Note the dates of each interpretation before you read it. The date may give you a clue to why Reconstruction was interpreted the way it was by each historian.

Historian A (1907, 1937)

(1) In the spring of 1865, the Southern armies surrendered bringing the Civil War to a close. To the people of the North, the Union had been preserved. To the people of the South, uncertainty and foreboding dominated. In some parts of the South the economy was almost at a standstill. Railways and bridges were destroyed, many farms lay idle, and worst of all, the system of labor was completely disorganized.

(2) Despite these drawbacks there was an opportunity for prompt recovery if the whole population, black as well as white, could have resumed plantation production, especially of cotton, since the price was fabulously high. But before such economic results were to be attained, Northern politicians plunged the South into political crises which paralyzed the region.

(3) "With malice toward none; with charity toward all," President Lincoln had said in March 1865. It was his policy toward the South. He realized the South had to be brought back into the Union without harsh restrictions.

[Continued on next page.]

Historian A

[Continued from previous page.]

After Lincoln's assassination, President Johnson continued the policy of encouraging Southern states to form governments under the generous 10% Plan.[1]

(4) Southerners were shocked and insulted by Negro troops in their midst, by being "jostled from the sidewalks by dusky guards" among whom, in some cases, they recognized their former servants.[2] There was no need for troops—the South had accepted defeat. Further, Southerners resented being commanded to ratify the 13th Amendment before they could reenter the Union. Despite these difficulties, the Southern states chose new governments and sent their representatives off to Washington. Their representatives were never allowed to sit in the government.

(5) Vindictive politicians, called Radical Republicans, prevented the Southern Senators and Representatives from taking their seats. Led by the sarcastic and scornful Thaddeus Stevens, the Radical Republicans wanted confiscation of ex–Confederate property, Negro suffrage (right to vote), and punishment of rebels. Stevens openly explained his motive by saying his policies "would insure the ascendancy of the Union [Republican] party."[3]

(6) The Radical Republicans used as the excuse for their harsh actions the so-called "Black Codes" of the seceded states. The Radicals claimed these laws, passed in Southern states, were an attempt by the reorganized governments to drive blacks back into virtual slavery. Actually, the Black Codes gave specific rights to blacks and were a straightforward attempt to bring order out of the chaos brought about by the war and emancipation of the slaves. The laws simply reflected the actual situation in the South. Freedmen were not, and could not be for generations, on the same social, moral and intellectual plane with whites, so they were accorded a separate class by law. The restrictions in respect to bearing arms, testifying in court, and keeping labor contracts were justified by well-established traits and habits of Negroes.[4]

(7) The worst problem was caused by the vagrancy of the Negroes. As soon as they received freedom, many blacks irresponsibly wandered around and did not work. Many became vagabonds, wandering from camp to camp and becoming unmanageable. Even a sympathizer with blacks said they strayed from the plantations "just at the time when their labor was most needed to secure the crops of the season."[5] Naturally, Southern states passed vagrancy laws as part of the Black Codes in order to stop this idleness and get the farms and plantations running again.

(8) But Northerners believed the Radical propaganda about Black Codes. The Radicals created the Freedmen's Bureau and passed a Civil Rights Law. The Freedmen's Bureau was a mixture of genuine service and shameful corruption. It's head, General O.O. Howard, was a man of the finest character, but many of its agents were unscrupulous and abused their powers. Southerners thoroughly disliked the agency.

(9) Like the Freedmen's Bureau, the Civil Rights Act was an unwarranted extension of central government power forced upon state governments. The Radicals argued that Negro rights were insecure unless protected by federal (national) law. They soon made the protection of Negro rights a part of the Constitution itself by passing the Fourteenth Amendment and getting it ratified.

[Continued on next page.]

Historian A

[Continued from previous page.]

(10) In 1867 the Radical program to control state governments in the South reached its peak when the Reconstruction Act was passed. This act divided 10 Southern states into 5 military districts and required general Negro enfranchisement (voting) and disfranchisement (denial of the right to vote) of many former rebels. The military commanders were to register the voters, assemble the conventions, and adopt new state constitutions—in short, start new state governments. The Southern states were now under the control of the Republican Party.

(11) For the Southern states this period of Republican control was the darkest time of Reconstruction. Northern "carpetbaggers" were now running the state governments. These dishonest politicians, so named because their few belongings could all fit into a small bag, came South to make money and gain political power. They allied themselves with Southern "scalawags," white Southern natives who took advantage of the situation to make money and gain power. Aided by a system which gave the vote to the Negro while it disfranchised the wealthier, more intelligent whites, the carpetbaggers and scalawags brought new levels of corruption and fraud to state government.

(12) Elections in the South became a joke. Ignorant blacks voted by the thousands without knowing even the names of the men for whom they were voting.[6] Vote-buying became so common that Negroes came to expect it; much of the bacon and ham mentioned as "relief" was given out with an eye to election-day results.[7] Starting early in the morning, Negro voters in Florida moved along in groups, voting at every polling place, each time under an assumed (fake) name.[8]

(13) The corruption and fraud were unbelievable. A congressional committee reported that one of the leading carpetbag governors made over $100,000 during his first year though his salary was $8,000.[9] Another carpetbag governor was charged with stealing and selling the food of the Freedmen's Bureau intended for the relief of helpless and ragged ex-slaves. F.J. Moses, scalawag, stated that he received $15,000 while governor of South Carolina for approving a large printing bill.[10]

(14) Radical Republican legislatures, supported by the army, piled up expenses against their poor states to fantastic heights. Millions of dollars were lent to railroads, increasing state debts beyond all reason. In Florida the cost of printing alone in 1869 was more than the entire cost of state government in 1860. Taxes, of course, rose dramatically. White women sold possessions and food needed for their hungry children in order to pay taxes. Many whites lost their land for failure to pay taxes, and the land was bought by Negroes and Northern carpetbaggers.[11]

(15) Needless to say, decent white men in the South detested this misgovernment. The resentment led to tension between the races which soon became violent. The Union Leagues provided a secret organization, including secret rites and ceremonies, that Negroes joined to terrorize whites.[12] In reaction, extremist whites formed the Ku Klux Klan, organized to use violence to intimidate blacks.

(16) At election times blacks were systematically terrorized to keep them away from the polls. As Northern troops were withdrawn from the South (the last troops were withdrawn in 1877)

[Continued on next page.]

Historian A

[Continued from previous page.]

conservative whites regained control of their state governments. Unfortunately, Radical rule in the South had embittered relations between blacks and whites for generations.

(17) Reconstruction was a tragic era in American history. In the name of protecting Negroes' rights, Radical Republicans imposed national control on the Southern states, completely ignoring the constitutional concept of federalism in which states should handle issues within their own boundaries. The fact that most Northern states did not give blacks the right to vote shows that Radicals were not really interested in blacks' rights. Rather, they used the blacks to gain political power for the Republican Party. The whole era was marked by this hypocrisy which hurt both whites and blacks in the South.

Historian A Endnotes

1   President Johnson spoke about harsh penalties on ex-Confederates but he nevertheless pardoned most of them and allowed new governments to be formed. The 10% Plan allowed the people of each state to organize a state government when 10% of the population took an oath to support the constitution of the United States in the future.

2   Whitelaw Reid, *After the War: A Southern Tour.* (Cincinnati, 1866) (quoting a New Orleans editorial), p. 422.

3   *Congressional Globe*, 39 Congress, 2 session, 252 (January 3, 1867).

4   W.L. Fleming, *Documentary History of Reconstruction.* (Cleveland, OH, 1906–7), Vol. I, p. 247.

5   Carl Schurz, *Reminiscences of Carl Schurz.* (New York, 1907–8) Vol. III, p. 214.

6   Fleming, Vol. II, p. 44. Statement of Samuel Hale, a Unionist (a Southerner who supported the North during the Civil War), in 1867, to a Congressional committee: "I wish you could have seen the poor, ignorant blacks giving in their 'bits of paper,' as they called their printed ballots, when they knew no more of the names on them...than you did."

7   Ibid., Vol. II, p. 83. Deputy U.S. Marshall Perrin testified: "[A] report was circulated among the Negroes that in order to obtain bacon they would have to vote the straight Republican ticket."

8   Ibid., Vol. II, pp. 85–86. Mr. Wallace, who was on the Republican side in the Florida election campaign described, stated in his book that blacks voted repeatedly.

9   Ibid., Vol. II, p. 39. Report of Messrs. Speer and Archer of the Congressional Investigating Committee in 1872. House Report no. 92, 42 Congress, 2nd Session, p. 24.

10 Ibid., Vol. II, p. 41. Statement by F.J. Moses in 1873, contained in *Report on Public Frauds in South Carolina*, p. 317.

11 F.B. Simkins and R.H. Woody, *South Carolina during Reconstruction.* (Chapel Hill, 1932), pp. 178–79.

12 Fleming, Vol. II, Chapter vii. Extracts from the *Ritual of the Union League of America* includes emblems such as altar, Bible, incense, sword, anvil and rites such as "Have I your solemn pledge to keep secret whatever may transpire in your presence?"

Historian B (1965)

(1) Reconstruction has been called a tragic era by traditional historians. According to this view, the Radical Republicans imposed control on the Southern states, setting up corrupt state governments under carpetbaggers, scalawags, and freedmen. Naturally, Southern whites resented this control and fought back as soon as they could. Thus, racial tensions in the South were strained. The economy of the South was

[Continued on next page.]

Historian B

[Continued from previous page.]

crippled and blacks did not get their rights.

(2) This traditional viewpoint greatly distorts what really happened during Reconstruction. The efforts of the Radical Republicans actually were idealistic and made Southern society more democratic in the long run. The short term problems were caused by Southern whites, not the Radicals. To be sure, there was some corruption in Reconstruction governments, and there were other problems. Nevertheless, the efforts of the Radicals helped blacks and show that the tragic era view is wrong.

(3) In 1865 President Lincoln wanted to bind the nation back together quickly by allowing Southerners to reorganize their state governments on generous terms in what became known as the 10% Plan. President Johnson continued Lincoln's policies and Southern states soon had their governments in place. Just as soon as those governments were in place, they passed "Black Codes" under which blacks were not allowed to marry whites, serve on juries, or testify against whites. In South Carolina, Negroes could work only as agricultural labor except with a special license. Mississippi would not permit Negroes to buy or rent farm land. And in a number of Southern states, Negroes found without lawful employment were to be arrested as vagrants and auctioned off or hired to landowners who would pay their fines. In Louisiana Negroes were not permitted to leave their place of employment without permission, and they could not refuse to work for their employers. Blacks were little better than slaves, since they could easily be tied to a plantation as cheap labor—they could not move around looking for other work for fear of being arrested under the vagrancy laws. Fur-

ther, they could not vote or go to school.[1]

(4) As might be expected, the Black Codes angered many Northerners. It was obvious to everyone that the future envisioned for the Negro by Southern whites was that of an illiterate, unskilled, propertyless, agricultural worker.[2] Those who cared about rights for blacks had no choice but to oppose the governments formed under the Johnson policies. Thus, when the Southern delegates showed up to sit in Congress, the Republicans refused to seat them. The truth is, and it is very important, that before the Radical Republican program began, the Johnson governments themselves had introduced the whole pattern of disfranchisement, discrimination, and segregation into the postwar South. These racist policies against Negroes weren't a response to Radical control—they happened first.

(5) The Radicals' motivation for fighting President Johnson over Reconstruction in the South has been a source of disagreement. Traditional historians see the Radicals as wanting revenge on Southerners and wanting to strengthen the Republican Party by getting the Negro vote. But the Radicals had been abolitionists before the Civil War, some for over 20 years. This shows their genuine concern for Negro rights. Why would they lose their idealism suddenly in 1865? The Radicals felt that the only way Negroes could learn to be free men was for them to start living as free men.

(6) Some Radicals wanted to give economic assistance to blacks in the form of land. Land ownership would give blacks the economic power to become independent of the plantation system. The land would be confiscated (taken from) the chief rebels (about 5% of Southern families) and divided among the freed-

[Continued on next page.]

Historian B

[Continued from previous page.]

men each of whom would receive "40 acres and a hut." Even most Radicals believed so strongly in private property, however, that they could not support taking land away from any owner. As an alternative, economic assistance was given through the Freedmen's Bureau. This agency was well run, but made many enemies in the South. The bureau provided emergency relief, set up Negro schools, prevented landowners from taking advantage of Negroes, and protected Negroes' civil rights.

(7) The conflict heightened between Johnson and the Radicals until Congress passed the Reconstruction Act of 1867 over Johnson's veto. In it, the South was divided into 5 military districts. Troops would now be used to ensure that blacks would be able to vote and enjoy their other rights as citizens. Southern state governments were now controlled by three groups—carpetbaggers, scalawags, and freedmen. Some carpetbaggers, it is true, were disreputable characters, but most were sincerely interested in helping blacks. They were mostly teachers and clergy. Scalawags have likewise been stereotyped as traitors looking for political power. In reality, they were made up of four different groups with very different motives. Their common feature was that they felt the Republican party would promote their political and economic interests.

(8) The third group in the Reconstruction governments was the freedmen. Most were illiterate and many were easily intimidated. They wanted suffrage (the right to vote) and, although they consistently voted Republican, they had their own leadership and were not always tools of the Republicans. They were seldom vengeful toward Southern whites.

(9) The new Republican state governments wrote very good state constitutions which contained a number of important reforms, such as free public education. There was definitely some corruption in the Radical governments. There were fraudulent bond issues and graft in the sale of land. Governor Warmoth allegedly pocketed $100,000 during his first year in office, though his salary was $8,000. Another governor was accused of stealing and selling the supplies of the Freedmen's Bureau. The credit of some Southern states was hurt by mounting debts.

(10) But the high taxes, mounting debts, and corruption of the Radical regimes must be put within the context of those times. The devastation of the Civil War required a great deal of spending to rebuild factories, bridges, and so forth no matter who was running the governments at the time. This was, moreover, a time of great corruption throughout the United States, as the incredible swindling by the Tweed Ring in New York City shows. Further, the reforms begun under the Radicals such as public education and relief for the destitute were costly, but were democratic and worthwhile.

(11) Most of the debt increases went for grants and loans to railroads, among whose owners were always some native white Democrats. And some Democrats always voted for railroad bond issues.[3] Most of Alabama's Reconstruction debt—$18,000,000 out of $20,500,000—was for state bonds issued to help railroad construction. Thus, very little of the money gained by corruption ended up in Negro pockets.

(12) To further complicate matters, when white Democrats took over in the 1870s, the Southern states often found

[Continued on next page.]

Historian B

[Continued from previous page.]

the new governments just as corrupt as before. The treasurer of one Democratic government embezzled $316,000 which broke all previous records. Eight other state treasurers were found guilty of embezzlement, including one in Louisiana who stole over a million dollars. In Mississippi, a white delegate said that, "We have been stuffing ballot boxes, committing perjury, and here and there in the state carrying the elections by fraud and violence....No man can be in favor of perpetuating the election methods which have prevailed in Mississippi since 1875 who is not a moral idiot."

(13) The real problem in Reconstruction governments was not corruption—corruption existed in Southern governments before and after Reconstruction. The real problem was the change in who paid taxes. Whites were now paying

their fair share of higher taxes and they were paying them for services provided to blacks.

(14) Eventually, Southern whites used violence to prevent blacks from voting which undermined Republican strength. The violence was epitomized by the Ku Klux Klan, but it continued as a basic part of Southern politics long after the Klan declined.[4] The Republican party was divided and support for the rights of blacks dwindled in the 1870s. When the final troops were withdrawn in 1877 blacks were left to the mercy of whites. Southern society was rigidly segregated and blacks had few rights for more than 70 years. Nevertheless, Reconstruction had seen the passage of the Fourteenth and Fifteenth Amendments which became key elements in the Civil Rights Movement of the 1950s and 1960s—the second Reconstruction.

Endnotes for Historian B

[1] Governor Humphreys of Mississippi affirmed in his inaugural address, "that ours is and it shall ever be, a government of white men." Carl Schurz, an observer in the South, stated that "the popular prejudice is almost as bitterly set against the Negro's having the advantage of education as it was when the Negro was a slave...Hundreds of times I heard the old assertion repeated that 'learning will spoil the nigger for work,' and 'Negro education will be the ruin of the South.'"

[2] A delegate to the Texas Constitutional Convention said: "I concede them [blacks] nothing but the station of 'hewers of wood and drawers of water.'"

[3] Ella Lonn, (a historian), *Reconstruction in Louisiana after 1868.* (New York, 1918), pp. 36–37. "Such measures [railroad bond issues] were supported by members of both parties, often introduced by Democrats, in every case supported by a large majority of Democrats in both houses."

[4] In the Mississippi campaign of 1875 a local newspaper announced, "All other means having been exhausted to abate the horrible conditions of things, the thieves and robbers, and scoundrels, white and black, deserve death and ought to be killed....Carry the election peaceably if we can, forcibly if we must."

Historian C (1988)

(1) The Civil War brought great changes to the United States. Blacks had fought valiantly on the Union side. "They say," an Alabama planter reported in 1867, "the Yankees never could have whipped the South without the aid of the Negroes." Military service along

with emancipation brought new status for blacks and new claims to equal citizenship.[1] The meeting of the national black convention at Syracuse in October 1864 criticized racial prejudice in the Northern states.

[Continued on next page.]

Historian C

[Continued from previous page.]

(2) The North prospered from the war. But the North was divided in many ways. Industrial businessmen were tied closely with the Republican party and a strong central government, including national paper currency and a national banking system. Skilled workers prospered from the war, but among the poorer classes there was great resentment as shown by the New York City draft riot of July 1863. It originated in resentment over the draft—the provision that men who paid $300 didn't have to serve in the army was called "class legislation." But it also showed resentment toward wealthy industrial owners, abolitionists, and blacks. The Colored Orphan Asylum was burned to the ground and countless blacks were beaten or murdered.[2]

(3) The South was devastated by the war. Like the North, it too was divided. Large sections of the hill country of Southern states hated the wealthy plantation owners and their "slaveocracy." They resented taxes, which were very low for the large plantation owners of the lowlands while the up-country farmers paid high taxes. And, of course, they resented the plantation owners for leading their states into the disastrous Civil War. The up-country contained many Unionist (pro–North) regions, the extreme being the hill country of Virginia which formed the separate state of West Virginia. Naturally, these Unionist strongholds supported the Republicans against traditional Southern leaders during Reconstruction.

(4) At the end of the war in the spring of 1865, many Southern whites assumed that blacks faced the end of slavery entirely unprepared for the responsibilities of freedom.[3] Blacks, however, had very specific ideas about freedom. They immediately held mass meetings and religious services and acquired dogs, guns, and liquor, all of which had been barred under slavery. Among the most resented of the restrictions under slavery was the rule that no black could travel without a pass. Now blacks moved in large numbers. Some moved to cities to get away from plantation labor. Many moved to be reunited with family members separated during slavery.[4] Blacks also withdrew their women and children from field labor. In 1869 a Georgia newspaper reported, "The Freedmen have almost universally withdrawn their women and children from the fields, putting the first at housework and the latter at school." In addition, freedmen set up their own churches, schools and benevolent societies (burial societies, debating clubs, fire companies, trade associations, and so forth).

(5) To blacks freedom meant freedom from working in gangs under the direction of an overseer, as they had under slavery. Further, as in other places where slavery was abolished, freedmen in the United States saw land ownership as the key to their economic independence.[5] They couldn't afford to buy the land so they asked the government to distribute land to them. They wanted small farms where they would grow food crops for subsistence rather than the "slave crops"—cotton. "If ole massa want to grow cotton, let him plant it himself," declared a Georgia freedman. And blacks demanded the right to vote.[6]

(6) Southern whites reacted sharply to blacks defining their freedom in so many ways. They often responded with violence when blacks did not treat them as superiors, or when there were labor disputes, such as attempting to leave plantations, arguing over labor con-

[Continued on next page.]

Historian C

[Continued from previous page.]

tracts, or resisting whippings.[7] Plantation owners, meanwhile, realized they needed black labor to continue their plantations. Emancipation in the West Indies taught the plantation owners an important lesson: freedmen must be barred from access to land. Only on smaller islands, like Barbados, where whites owned all the land, "and the Negro is unable to get possession of a foot of it," had plantation agriculture continued to prosper. Plantation owners turned to written contracts with freedmen to reestablish their authority over every aspect of their laborers' lives.

(7) The disputes between white owners and black workers were intensified by nature. Poor weather in 1866 caused a poor crop at the same time that the price of cotton plummeted.[8]

(8) Into this crucial situation stepped Andrew Johnson. When O.O. Howard, the head of the Freedmen's Bureau, issued an order to set aside forty-acre tracts of land for freedmen (the Bureau controlled over 850,000 acres of abandoned lands) the President made him issue a new order restoring almost all of the land to its former white owners. Thousands of freedmen were evicted (thrown out) from the land they had "owned." Johnson further recognized the new Southern state governments, though none of them gave the vote to blacks, and he pardoned almost all ex-Confederates and restored their land to them. Johnson's pro-white policies encouraged white Southerners to resist civil rights, especially the vote, for blacks.

(9) The "slaveocracy" was back in power in the South. Property taxes were kept low while freedmen and poor whites paid a much higher portion of their income in taxes. Though both blacks and whites paid taxes, services (such as poor relief and education) were provided for whites which were not provided for blacks.[9] Plantation owners used state governments to enforce labor discipline. State and local governments passed laws limiting black freedom of movement, punishing them for vagrancy (a vagrant is someone who isn't working when he should be) and restricting blacks' right to rent or buy land. The Black Codes forced blacks to sign labor contracts and punished those who did not stick to them. Mississippi required all blacks to have, each January, written evidence of employment for the coming year. Laborers leaving their jobs before the contract expired would forfeit wages already earned and could be arrested.

(10) Quite naturally, Republicans rejected Johnson's policies in the South, including the Black Codes. Radical Republicans, such as Thaddeus Stevens, had fought for decades to free the slaves. Now he and many moderate Republicans were asking if the slaves had been freed only to have no rights. In the Congressional Joint Committee on Reconstruction, speaker after speaker criticized Johnson's lenient policies toward ex-Confederates for encouraging whites to resist granting blacks' rights. They told of injustices against blacks, loyal whites, and Northerners. One black stated, "If [Southern] representatives were received in Congress, the condition of the freedmen would be very little better than that of the slaves."[10] The Southern representatives chosen under Johnson's policies were not allowed in Congress.

(11) Congress then passed the Freedmen's Bureau Bill and the Civil Rights Bill, both of which Johnson vetoed. Congress overrode his vetoes and then passed the Fourteenth Amendment. The

[Continued on next page.]

Historian C

[Continued from previous page.]

United States alone among the nations that abolished slavery in the nineteenth century clothed its former slaves with citizenship rights equal to those of whites. After the 1866 Election, Congress passed the Reconstruction Act which divided the South into 5 military districts and required suffrage for blacks and ratification of the Fourteenth Amendment. New governments under Republican control were soon established in the Southern states.

(12) The new Reconstruction governments consisted of a few Northerners (a small minority since Northerners were less than 2 percent of the Southern population); Southern whites, the largest group, which controlled the party in the South; and the freedmen. The Northerners, called carpetbaggers by Southerners, were mostly veterans of the Civil War, teachers, Freedmen's Bureau agents, and investors in cotton plantations. Most of these Northerners probably combined the desire for personal gain with a commitment to remake Southern society based on freedom.[11]

(13) Southern whites who supported the Republican party, called scalawags by conservative whites, were made up of many different groups. But most of them were from up-country areas which were Unionist during the Civil War. These white Republicans disagreed on many issues, but they agreed in trying to take power away from the slaveocracy, as we have seen. They wanted low taxes and a public school system. They were committed to blacks' civil rights but the commitment was shaky. Blacks were concentrated in the lowland plantation areas. If plantation owners could control the black vote, the lowlands would be stronger and the up-country would be weaker. Besides, racism was a central part of their upbringing.

(14) Blacks comprised the third group of Republicans. They joined the Union Leagues hoping for land, and almost all of them voted.[12] They had a junior role in the Republican Party, however, which they came to resent and against which they spoke out.

(15) The new Republican governments in the South wrote modern liberal constitutions, including state-funded systems of free public education; guaranteed civil and political rights for blacks; and abolition of such things as property qualifications for holding office, imprisonment for debt, and whipping as a punishment for crime.[13] But the new governments faced a crisis of legitimacy. Ordinarily, political parties take for granted the authority of the government and the legitimacy of the other parties. Reconstruction opponents, however, viewed the new governments as foreign—forced on them from outside. They felt blacks were not entitled to a permanent role in politics. Thus, Republican governments depended upon winning over white voters for their very existence. Compromises made by white Republicans at the expense of blacks were made from the start.

(16) The Reconstruction governments had major expenses to pay for rebuilding the South from the devastation of the war. Republicans as well as Democrats believed that railroads generated prosperity.[14] In the first years of Republican rule, every Southern state gave lavish aid to railroad companies. Soon the extensive borrowing caused the credit of the state governments to collapse. Widespread corruption further drained the state treasuries and undermined the legitimacy of the Republicans. The corruption was not unique to these governments, however, and

[Continued on next page.]

Historian C

[Continued from previous page.]

Democrats, especially railroad owners, shared in the spoils. In fact, although blacks were involved in the corruption, they received very little from it.[15] Political involvement often made their lives much worse.

(17) Blacks never did get the land they hoped for, though large tracts of land were confiscated for nonpayment of taxes. Further, the Democrats used the race issue to divide the Republicans. At every opportunity Democrats forced white Republicans to take a position on racial questions such as interracial marriage and separate schools for blacks and whites. If the Republicans sided with blacks they would lose white votes. Southerners also resorted to violence to intimidate and disfranchise (prevent from voting) blacks. As we have seen, violence was common throughout Reconstruction. After the start of Republican governments, however, it was increased dramatically by such organizations as the Ku Klux Klan. The Klan aimed to destroy the Republican party in the South, reestablish control of the black labor force, and restore the racial subordination of blacks in every aspect of Southern life.[16]

(18) The Republican party in the North was weakened by political struggles over economic and political issues, such as corruption in the Grant Administration. Support in the North for blacks' rights had always been limited anyway, as shown by the defeat of black suffrage in all the Northern states outside New England except for Iowa and Minnesota.[17] Racism was a part of Northern society, as was shown above in the New York City draft riot. Northern investors wanted Southern plantations to produce cash crops, especially cotton, which would promote economic growth. Thus, they too were concerned that freedmen

be disciplined workers on productive plantations. They gave little support to black ownership of small farms, and as capitalists they vehemently opposed confiscating land from ex-Confederates to divide it among freedmen.[18] The Republican party became increasingly allied to these capitalists through the 1860s and 1870s.

(19) The depression of 1873 weakened the Republican party in the North. The working class became critical of railroad owners and other capitalists. Reconstruction governments in the South were crippled as up-country farmers as well as planters were squeezed by falling cotton prices. Prejudice and violence against blacks intensified once again.[19] By 1877 all the Southern states were "redeemed" from Republican control. Conservative white Democrats were again running Southern governments while most blacks no longer voted or participated in politics. The great experiment in Reconstruction was over.

(20) In terms of its goal of securing blacks' rights as citizens and free laborers, Reconstruction can only be judged a failure. A number of reasons for this outcome seem especially significant. The weather and the depression of 1873 severely limited the chances for basic economic changes. Political conflicts in the North and a variety of competing interests in the South divided the Republican Party. Corruption further undermined the legitimacy of the Reconstruction governments. The decision by almost all groups to reject giving land to the freedmen kept the land, and hence a great deal of economic power, in the hands of the plantation owners. Racism in both the North and South severely limited white commitments to blacks' rights. Another key to the failure was

[Continued on next page.]

Historian C

[Continued from previous page.]

the campaign of violence that returned the South to the hands of the Democrats.

(21) Blacks and Radical Republicans had envisioned an expanded role for the national government in protecting the fundamental rights of American citizens. Most whites would not agree with such an interventionist government. Nevertheless, most did not oppose the use of the army to pursue the Nez Perce Indians to enforce a federal order, or the use of the army to protect private property against striking workers in the Great Railroad Strike of 1877. The inconsistencies of Americans' beliefs, and the conflicting interests between various groups, went a long way toward explaining the failures of Reconstruction.

Endnotes for Historian C

1 Former slave William Murphey at the Arkansas constitutional convention of 1868 asked: "Has not the man who conquers upon the field of battle, gained any rights? Have we gained none by the sacrifice of our brethren?"

2 Mattie Griffeth to Mary Estlin, (letter) July 27, 1863, Estlin Papers, Dr. William's Library, London:

> "A child of 3 years of age was thrown from a 4th story window and instantly killed. A woman one hour after confinement was set upon and beaten with her tender babe in arms....Children were torn from their mother's embrace and their brains blown out in the very face of the afflicted mother. Men were burnt by slow fires."

3 South Carolinian White Julius Fleming wrote, "The Negroes are to be pitied....They do not understand the liberty which has been conferred upon them."

4 John W. De Forest, *A Union Officer in the Reconstruction*, edited by James Croushere and David Potter. (New Haven, 1948), pp. 36–37. De Forest, who was a Freedmen's Bureau agent wrote: "In their eyes the work of emancipation was incomplete until the families which had been dispersed by slavery were reunited."

5 Edward Magdol, *A Right to the Land: Essays on the Freedmen's Community*. (Westport, CT, 1977), pp. 140–41. Magdol says that freedmen in Haiti, the British and Spanish Caribbean, and Brazil all wanted land ownership.

6 At the statewide conventions in the South in 1865 speaker after speaker from the black delegation called for universal manhood suffrage (every male being able to vote regardless of race or property holdings).

7 39th Congress, 1st Session, House Report 30, pt. 2:178

A Freedmen's Bureau agent stated that, "Southern whites are quite indignant if they are not treated with the same deference that they were accustomed to" under slavery.

Barry A. Crouch, "A Spirit of Lawlessness: White Violence, Texas Blacks, 1865–1868," *Journal of Social History*, 18 (Winter 1984), pp. 218–20. This article details violence over labor disputes.

8 George Benham, *A Year of Wreck*. (New York, 1980), pp. 402–3.

Benham, a Northern planter, stated, "If Providence had smiled on this region in 1866, by giving it a reasonable crop,...injustice to the Negro and the newcomer, bitterness of heart and hatred of the government would all have disappeared. In the absence of a good crop...all these were intensified."

9 Howard Rabinowitz, "From Exclusion to Segregation: Southern Race Relations, 1865–1890," *Journal of American History*, 63 (September 1976), pp. 326–27.

"Southern states and cities barred blacks from poor relief, orphanages, parks, and schools among others."

10 39th Congress, 1st Session, House Report 30, pt. 2: pp. 30–31, 55–56.

11 William C. Harris, "The Creed of the Carpetbaggers: The Case of Mississippi," *Journal of Southern History* 40 (May 1974), pp. 199–224.

[Continued on next page.]

Endnotes for Historian C
[Continued from previous page.]

[12] Cincinnati *Commercial* in *American Freedman*, February 1868, p. 373.

[13] Jean-Charles Houzeau, *My Passage at the New Orleans "Tribune": A Memoir of the Civil War*, edited by David C. Rankin, translated by Gerard F. Debault. (Baton Rouge, 1984), p. 143.

Tribune editor Houzeau said that most of the conventions produced modern, democratic constitutions, "magnificent for their liberal principles."

The texts of the Reconstruction constitutions are in Francis N. Thorpe, ed., *The Federal and State Constitutions*, 7 vols (Washington, D.C., 1909).

[14] Mark W. Summers, *Railroads, Reconstruction, and the Gospel of Prosperity: Aid Under the Radical Republicans, 1865–1877*. (Princeton, 1984), pp. 68–84.

[15] Edmund Drago, *Black Politicians and Reconstruction in Georgia*. (Baton Rouge, 1982), p. 67.

[16] Allen W. Trelease, *White Terror: The Ku Klux Klan Conspiracy and Southern Reconstruction*. (New York, 1971), p. xlvi.

[17] William Gillette, *The Right to Vote*. (Baltimore, 1969 ed.), pp. 25–28.

[18] *New York Times*, February 19, March 10, April 10, June 27, 1867.

When Thaddeus Stevens submitted a bill giving 40 acres to freedmen from confiscated land, conservative Republicans denounced Stevens for adding to "the distrust which already deters capitalists" from investing in the South. The *New York Times* said that capitalists would not invest for fear of confiscation.

[19] 44th Congress, 2nd Session, Senate Miscellaneous Document 48, 1:34–39, 3:473–76; Daniel Henderson, *The White Man's Revolution in South Carolina*. (North Augusta, S.C., 1916), p. 1.

An example of white violence occurred in the town of Hamburg, South Carolina, in 1874. A dispute developed between black militia and armed whites. Outgunned, the black militia tried to flee. Twenty-five were captured by whites, of which five were murdered in cold blood. After the killings, a white mob ransacked the homes and the shops of the town's blacks.

 ## Historian A

1. What is the main point of Historian A's view?

2. How does Historian A view each of the following? (Hint: watch for adjectives)

   a. Radical Republicans

   b. Former Confederates and plantation owners

[Continued on next page.]

[Continued from previous page.]

  c. Freedmen

  d. Carpetbaggers

  e. Scalawags

3. What group was primarily responsible for the failure of Reconstruction, according to Historian A? Explain your answer.

4. Evaluate the evidence in the following.
  a. Endnote 6

  b. Endnote 8

  c. Endnote 10

5. Identify and evaluate the reasoning used in the following.
  a. Paragraph 14

[Continued on next page.]

©1991 MIDWEST PUBLICATIONS/CRITICAL THINKING PRESS & SOFTWARE, P.O. BOX 448, PACIFIC GROVE, CA 93950 47

[Continued from previous page.]

    b. Paragraph 15

    c. Third sentence of paragraph 17

Q Historian B

6.   What is Historian B's main point?

7.   How does Historian B view each of the following?
    a. Radical Republicans

    b. Former Confederates and plantation owners

    c. Freedmen

    d. Carpetbaggers

[Continued on next page.]

[Continued from previous page.]

    e. Scalawags

8. Which group does Historian B primarily blame for the failures of Reconstruction? Explain your answer.

9. Evaluate the evidence in the following.

    a. Endnote 1

    b. Endnote 2

    c. Endnote 4

10. Identify and evaluate the reasoning used in the following.

    a. Paragraph 2

    b. Paragraph 3, eighth sentence ("Blacks were little better...")

    c. Paragraph 4, last sentence

[Continued on next page.]

[Continued from previous page.]

    d. Paragraph 12, first sentence, and beyond for details

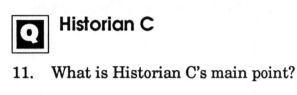 **Historian C**

11.   What is Historian C's main point?

12.   How does Historian C view each of the following?
    a. Radical Republicans

    b. Former Confederates and plantation owners

    c. Freedmen

    d. Carpetbaggers

    e. Scalawags

[Continued on next page.]

[Continued from previous page.]

13. Which group does Historian C primarily blame for the failure of Reconstruction? Explain your answer.

14. Evaluate the evidence in the following.

    a. Endnote 3

    b. Endnote 7, House Report

    c. Endnote 16

15. Identify and evaluate the reasoning used in the following.

    a. Paragraph 2

    b. Paragraph 5, second sentence

    c. Paragraph 10, second sentence

    d. Paragraph 20

[Continued on next page.]

[Continued from previous page.]

 General Questions

16. How do you think the time period in which they were written may have influenced each of the three histories of Reconstruction? (The dates of their publication are at the start of each interpretation.)

    Historian A

    Historian B

    Historian C

17. Label each statement below with the letter(s) of the historian(s) (**A**, **B**, or **C**) that would agree with it. Write more than one letter if you think more than one historian would agree. Write **N** if you think none of the historians would agree.

    _____ a.   Rich people should pay their fair share of taxes.

    _____ b.   Social arrangements between groups have a great influence on politics.

    _____ c.   Blacks are inferior to whites.

    _____ d.   All groups, no matter how poor or weak, have their own political goals which influence the outcome of events.

    _____ e.   Segregation is wrong.

    _____ f.   The government has the right to take land away from owners in the name of justice.

    _____ g.   Federal intervention into the affairs of states to protect rights of citizens is wrong.

    _____ h.   Only men of property and education should vote.

    _____ i.   Blacks played a very significant role in shaping the issues and outcomes of Reconstruction.

    _____ j.   Economic goals have great influence on people's beliefs and actions.

LESSON 8 What Does Visual Evidence Show about Reconstruction Attitudes toward Blacks?

After the Civil War the North faced some difficult questions. On what terms should the Southern states be allowed back into the Union? Should ex-Confederates be punished? Should Northern troops stay in the South and, if so, for how long? One of the most difficult questions concerned the freedmen: To what extent should the North interfere in the Southern states to protect the rights of blacks?

The Republican Party tended to get more involved in protecting the rights of freedmen than did other groups. *Harper's Weekly* and its artist, Thomas Nast, were widely recognized as staunch supporters of Republicanism. Look at the drawings on the next three pages (pp. 54–56) and then answer the questions below.

 Note the date of publication of each drawing for clues as to what might have been happening at the time. Note also any symbols or labels in the cartoons.

1. What was the viewpoint of each of the drawings toward blacks? How did the perspective change? Write your answers here.

   Drawing 1–

   Drawing 2–

   Drawing 3–

2. Why did views of blacks change from 1865 to 1868 to 1874?

[Continued on next page.]

AUGUST 5, 1865.]   HARPER'S WEEKLY.   489

FRANCHISE.
AND NOT THIS MAN?"

The Library of Congress Collections

"THIS IS A WHITE MAN'S GOVERNMENT."

The Library of Congress Collections

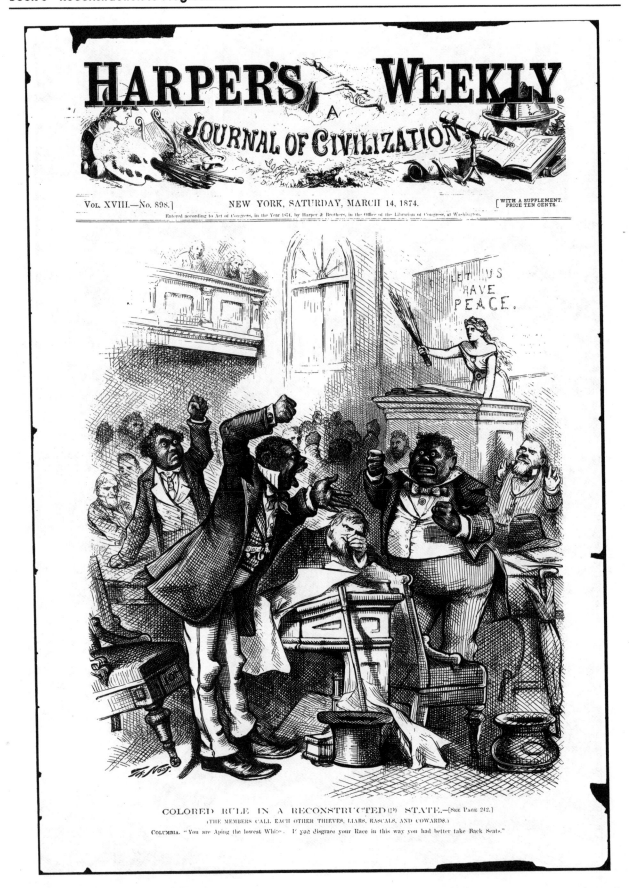

LESSON 9   Why Was the Fourteenth Amendment Passed?

After the Civil War the country confronted the task of reunification. Presidents Lincoln and Johnson took a generous position toward the defeated Confederates. Republicans in Congress were concerned about the rights of freedmen. The Republicans were made up basically of two groups, Moderates and Radicals. Most Radicals had been abolitionists before the Civil War. With the Emancipation Proclamation and the passage of the Thirteenth Amendment the dream of abolition became a reality.

This lesson is about the Fourteenth Amendment which was first introduced into Congress in December 1865 and passed by both houses of Congress by the necessary two-thirds majority in June 1866. It was then sent to the states for ratification. The question of ratification will not be dealt with in this lesson. Rather, the lesson will deal with the question of why the Fourteenth Amendment was passed in the form it was.

This lesson is in two parts. First, read the amendment and answer questions 1–3. Then read the sequence of proposals and the Relevant Information and answer the rest of the questions.

Fourteenth Amendment

Section 1. All persons born or naturalized in the United States and subject to the jurisdiction thereof, are citizens of the United States and of the State wherein they reside. No State shall make or enforce any law which shall abridge the privileges or immunities of citizens of the United States; nor shall any State deprive any person of life, liberty, or property, without due process of law; nor deny to any person within its jurisdiction the equal protection of the laws.

Section 2. Representatives shall be apportioned among the several States according to their respective numbers, counting the whole number of persons in each State, excluding Indians not taxed. But when the right to vote at any election for the choice of electors for President and Vice-President of the United States, Representatives in Congress, the Executive and Judicial officers of a State, or the members of the Legislature thereof, is denied to any of the male inhabitants of such State, being twenty-one years of age, and citizens of the United States, or in any way abridged, except for participation in rebellion, or other crime, the basis of representation therein shall be reduced in the proportion which the number of such male citizens shall bear to the whole number of male citizens twenty-one years of age in such State.

Section 3. No person shall be a Senator or Representative in Congress, or elector of President and Vice-President, or hold any office, civil or military, under the United States, or under any State, who, having previously taken an oath, as a

Fourteenth Amendment

[Continued from previous page.]

member of Congress, or as an officer of the United States, or as a member of any State legislature, or as an executive or judicial officer of any State, to support the Constitution of the United States, shall have engaged in insurrection or rebellion against the same, or given aid or comfort to the enemies thereof. But Congress may by a vote of two-thirds of each House, remove such disability.

Section 4. The validity of the public debt of the United States, authorized by law, including debts incurred for payment of pensions and bounties for services in suppressing insurrection or rebellion, shall not be questioned. But neither the United States nor any State shall assume or pay any debt or obligation incurred in aid of insurrection or rebellion against the United States, or any claim for the loss or emancipation of any slave; but all such debts, obligations and claims shall be held illegal and void.

Section 5. The Congress shall have power to enforce, by appropriate legislation, the provisions of this article.

 Questions

1. Why do you think Congress passed this amendment to the Constitution? Why didn't they just pass a law?

2. Why do you think in Section 2 that the option to deny the vote to any male citizen 21 years of age was given to the States? Why didn't the Congress just say that the vote could not be denied?

3. What two groups would probably have been very upset by this amendment?

[Continued on next page.]

[Continued from previous page.]

Now read the "Sequence of Proposals in Congress on the Fourteenth Amendment" and the Relevant Information and answer the questions that follow. Look back at the text of the Fourteenth Amendment (pp. 57–58) as needed to answer the questions.

Sequence of Proposals in Congress on the Fourteenth Amendment

I. Throughout 1865 and 1866 Radical Republicans proposed that blacks be given the right to vote in the Fourteenth Amendment. (As in the Fifteenth Amendment: "The right of citizens of the United States to vote shall not be denied or abridged by the United States or any State on account of race, color, or previous condition of servitude.") The proposal was defeated.

II. In January 1866 a proposal was made to base representation in the House of Representatives and Electoral College on the number of qualified voters in each state. The proposal was defeated.

III. At the end of January 1866 a proposal was submitted declaring that when a state denied any citizen the right to vote because of race, all members of that race would be excluded from the count to determine the number of representatives from that state. The proposal was defeated in the Senate

IV. At the end of April, an amendment combining civil rights (Section 1) with restriction of representation for denying the right to vote to any male inhabitants (Section 2) was sent to Congress by a House committee. The Amendment also included a third clause excluding from voting in national elections until 1870 those who had voluntarily aided the Confederacy, a fourth clause prohibiting payment of the Confederate debt, and a fifth clause empowering Congress to enforce the provisions of the amendment through legislation.

V. In May 1866 the Senate changed Section 3 to its present form in the amendment. The other four sections remained the same as in the House Committee amendment described in "IV" above. On June 13, 1866, Congress gave final approval to the amendment in this form. All Republicans voted for the amendment and all Democrats voted against it.

Relevant Information

A. In the *Dred Scott* case of 1857, the Supreme Court ruled that since blacks were not citizens when the Constitution was written, they were not protected by the Constitution. Therefore, Dred Scott did not have the right to sue in court.

B. In 1865 the President vetoed the Civil Rights Bill which gave blacks rights as citizens of the United States. Congress overrode the veto, so the bill became law.

C. At a later point in history a majority in Congress could pass a law wiping out the Civil Rights Act.

[Continued on next page.]

[Continued from previous page.]

D. Before the Civil War, three-fifths of the South's slaves counted toward calculating the number of representatives in Congress. Now, as free persons, all would be counted (though few were actually being allowed to vote) which would significantly increase the number of Southern representatives in the House of Representatives and the Electoral College. One Congressman predicted that if the system wasn't changed, ex-Confederates in alliance with Northern Democrats would gain control of Congress, give money to slave owners for the slaves they had freed, and elect Robert E. Lee president in 1868.

E. In the Constitution, representation in the House of Representatives and the Electoral College is based on the population, not the voters, of each state. The Electoral College is the body that chooses the President.

F. In 1866 New England had a higher percentage of women than did the western states. The North had more unnaturalized foreigners (people who couldn't vote) than did the West or South.

G. Passing literacy tests and meeting property qualifications in order to vote were common practices used by states to prevent poor people from voting.

H. Feminists such as Susan B. Anthony and Elizabeth Cady Stanton had allied themselves with the abolitionist movement before the Civil War. During the war, the women's movement had stopped pushing for the right to vote in order to help the Union and work for emancipation for blacks.

I. Before the Civil War many people believed in the states' rights view of government. They believed that states should determine what would happen to the citizens within their boundaries. The national government should not interfere with state governments. The states' rights view was crippled by the Civil War. The national government had not only fought a successful war against eleven states, the power of the national government had grown in the North also, especially in its dealings with business. Taxes had been imposed and a national banking system had been established. The Republican Party was most closely identified with these expanded powers of the national government. Nevertheless, many members of Congress wanted to be careful that the national government didn't become too powerful.

J. The year 1866 was an election year for Congress.

K. Radical Republicans had long pushed for the concept of equality before the law, overseen by the national government.

L. Democrats wanted the terms in the amendment to be defined with precision. What rights did the sponsors intend the amendment to protect?

M. Most Northern states did not allow blacks to vote.

N. Congress expanded the power of the federal (national) courts to try cases involving restrictions of rights protected in the Federal Constitution. Thus, the federal judiciary was given the task of defining what constituted a denial of "due process of law" or "equal protection of the laws." (Section 1, page 57)

[Continued on next page.]

[Continued from previous page.]

O.   In 1866 two riots broke out—one in Memphis in May and one in New Orleans in August. In the Memphis riot, 46 blacks were killed, 80 wounded, and at least 5 women raped. Over $100,000 worth of black property was destroyed or stolen. In New Orleans, 48 blacks were killed and 68 severely wounded. A Congressional committee report described the Memphis riot as "an organized and bloody massacre of the colored people."

P.   James Madison had said around the time of the adoption of the Constitution that although some states had written very good bills of rights "...there are others whose bills of rights are not only defective, but absolutely improper...."

Q.   In 1833 the Supreme Court ruled in *Barron v. Baltimore* that the protections in the first eight amendments of the Bill of Rights only protected citizens against the national government, not state governments.

R.   In May 1865 there was a struggle in the American Anti-Slavery Society. William Lloyd Garrison wanted to disband (end) the Society since slavery had ended. Wendell Phillips wanted the Society to push for political equality for freedmen, specifically the black vote. Elizabeth Cady Stanton and other women's rights activists supported Phillips, who won the vote and became the new president of the Society.

S.   The leader of the American Anti-Slavery Society, Wendell Phillips, told women's rights activists that they should all work for an amendment that would prevent disfranchisement (not allowing people to vote) on the grounds of race, color, or previous condition (slavery). "I hope," he added, "in time to be as bold as Stuart Mill and add to that last clause 'sex'!! But this hour belongs to the Negro. As Abraham Lincoln said 'One war at a time'; so I say, one question at a time. This hour belongs to the Negro." He refused to mix the two movements because "such a mixture would lose for the Negro far more than we should gain for the woman."

T.   Elizabeth Cady Stanton wrote a letter in reply to Phillips' speech (in S). "My question is this: Do you believe the African race is composed entirely of males?"

U.   Frances Gage wrote about the abolitionists who felt that this was the Negro's hour, "Can anyone tell us why the great advocates of Human Equality...forget that when they were a weak party [before the Civil War] and needed all the womanly strength of the nation to help them on, they always united the words 'without regards to sex, race or color?' Who ever hears of sex now from any of these champions of freedom?"

V.   In May 1866 a women's rights convention was held in New York City in which it adopted a platform favoring universal suffrage and forming the American Equal Rights Association to push for black and female suffrage at the same time.

[Continued on next page.]

[Continued from previous page.]

 Questions

4. Why weren't blacks simply given the vote as Radicals suggested in Proposal I?

5. Why were the civil rights of citizens made part of the Constitution instead of just being left as a law?

6. What was the point of Proposal II?

7. Why was Proposal II defeated?

[Continued on next page.]

[Continued from previous page.]

8.   Why was Proposal III defeated?

9.   What was the point of inserting "male" into the amendment in Proposal IV? What problems did it cause? Why was it done anyway?

10. What effect do you think the race riots (Relevant Information O) had on the Fourteenth Amendment?

11. What effects do you think the Fourteenth Amendment had?

LESSON 10   Evaluating Evidence

Part A

 Judge the following evidence according to the questions below.

1. Bill and Terry are the only two people in the jewelry section of the store when some jewelry is discovered missing. The security guard stops them and asks Bill if he stole the jewelry. Bill says, "No, it was Terry."

   a. Does Bill have a reason to lie?

   b. Is Bill a primary or secondary source?

   c. Is there other evidence supporting Bill's view?

   d. How reliable is Bill's evidence?

   e. How could you check on it further?

2. Ida Tarbell (a writer during Rockefeller's time) criticized Rockefeller for being immoral and hurting the country. Rockefeller said he never did anything immoral and he helped the country by eliminating wasteful competition.

   a. Does Rockefeller have a reason to lie?

   b. Who has more reason to lie, Rockefeller or Tarbell?

   c. Is Rockefeller a primary source?

[Continued on next page.]

[Continued from previous page.]

    d. Is Tarbell a primary source?

    e. Is there other evidence here supporting Rockefeller's view?

    f. Is Rockefeller's or Tarbell's evidence more reliable? Why?

    g. How could you check on this evidence further?

Part B

 Evaluate the following pieces of evidence by listing their strengths and weaknesses.

3.   Gwen told the coach she had done all the drills and the running suggested in preparation for the first day of practice.

        STRENGTHS   WEAKNESSES

4.   Andrew Carnegie said in his autobiography that he never produced anything unless it was the very best he could. He said he never knew of a successful business that did not do good, honest work.

        STRENGTHS   WEAKNESSES

[Continued on next page.]

[Continued from previous page.]

5. Gustavus Myers wrote in his book *The History of the Great American Fortunes,* published in 1936, that Jay Gould (1836–1892) was so corrupt that his name became associated with base crime and greed.

    STRENGTHS   WEAKNESSES

6. According to John Moody in his book *The Truth About Trusts* (1904), J.P. Morgan formed the largest corporation in the world in 1901 in US Steel. James E. Bruner in his book *Industrialism* also says US Steel was the largest corporation.

    STRENGTHS   WEAKNESSES

7. Henry Ford said in his book *My Life and Work* (1922) that he decided in 1909 to build only one model of the Ford car and that was the "Model T."

    STRENGTHS   WEAKNESSES

LESSON 11   Identifying and Evaluating Comparisons

Identifying Comparisons

Remember cue words for comparison reasoning, such as "like," "similar," "better," "worse," and so forth. Even without cue words, watch for items which compare two or more things. If you need help, look at the section on **comparisons** in the "Guide to Critical Thinking" (Unit 1).

Q Label each item below with the appropriate letter.

C   The item involves **comparison** reasoning.

N   The item does **not** involve comparison reasoning.

_____1.   We had over 50 pages to read last night for homework out of *To Kill a Mockingbird*.

_____2.   The Supreme Court has to decide about the capital punishment case during this session.

_____3.   I recommend you see *American Hero*. It was rated 4 stars and I'm sure you'd like it more than *Horror on Oak Street*.

_____4.   America's GNP rose from $165 per person in 1869–73 to $231 per person in 1897–1901.

_____5.   America's farmers had a lot of problems in the late 1800s. Farm machinery helped them produce a great deal but prices were low, so the farmers were in debt.

_____6.   J.P. Morgan's first major contribution to American industry was to help reorganize many of the country's railroads.

_____7.   During the depression of 1873, a number of private charitable organizations set up "soup houses" (soup kitchens) to feed the poor.

_____8.   America's farmers had a lot of problems in the late 1800s. Farm machinery increased production tremendously between 1860 and 1900, but prices declined even faster.

Evaluating Comparisons

The more similarities the better the comparison, in general.

The key question for evaluating comparisons is:

How are the two cases similar and how are they different?

[Continued on next page.]

[Continued from previous page.]

Q Use the key question for comparisons to evaluate each of the comparisons below.

9. This U.S. History course is a lot harder than the European History course. There is a lot more homework, and the tests are essay rather than multiple choice.

10. The United States could absorb so many immigrants in the 1800s while England could not because the United States had so much more land than England.

LESSON 12   Identifying and Evaluating Cause-and-Effect Reasoning

Identifying Cause-and-Effect Reasoning

In order to be cause-and-effect reasoning, a statement has to argue that something caused, led to, or brought about something else.

Q Label each item below with the appropriate letter.

C   The item uses **cause-and-effect** reasoning.

N   The item does **not** use cause-and-effect reasoning.

_____1.   The Cincinnati Reds are in first place due to their excellent relief pitching.

_____2.   The AAA maps helped us pick out the fastest route between New Orleans and Omaha.

_____3.   John D. Rockefeller was the richest of the American industrialists between 1865 and 1910.

_____4.   England was the first country to experience the industrial revolution. The United States did not begin industrializing until the mid-1800s.

_____5.   Industrialization increased the gap between rich and poor in the United States after the Civil War.

_____6.   In 1912 the Pujo Committee investigated J.P. Morgan's control of American business.

Evaluating Cause-and-Effect Reasoning

Q Evaluate the following cause-and-effect arguments. Refer to the section on **cause-and-effect** reasoning in the "Guide to Critical Thinking." Note especially the questions for evaluating cause and effect. Make a diagram of each argument, if necessary.

7.   There were a number of factors favorable to industrial growth in America in the years after the Civil War: many resources; a large labor supply; people with money to invest; no tariffs between states, so a large market for trade; many

[Continued on next page.]

[Continued from previous page.]

people willing to take the risks of starting new businesses; and a good nationwide transportation system.

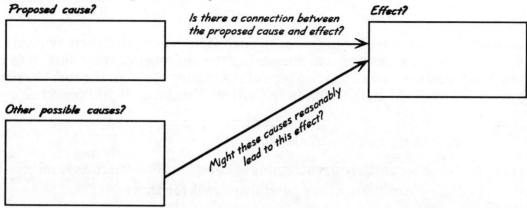

8. The depression of the 1870s hurt railroads in the United States a great deal. As shippers went bankrupt the railroads had to compete for fewer customers. This forced them to reduce rates. They tried to cut costs to compensate, but rates declined too far and many railroads went bankrupt, many more than in the late 1860s and early 1870s.

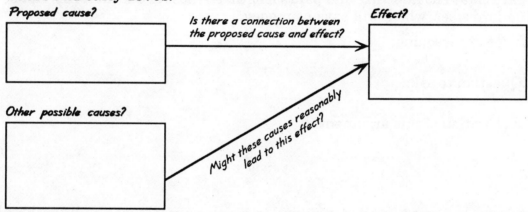

9. Industrialization ruined most artisans (a person skilled at making products involving a high level of workmanship). Since machines made products cheaply, artisans could not compete in terms of prices. The men running the machines were highly specialized, so they obviously could not make the whole product. That is, they were not artisans.

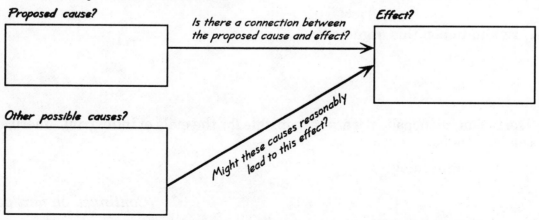

LESSON 13   Identifying and Analyzing Types of Reasoning

 Identify the type of reasoning used in each item below and then evaluate that type of reasoning by asking and answering the appropriate question(s). In those items that contain more than one type of reasoning, focus on the most important type. Read pp. 7–11 in the "Guide to Critical Thinking" if you need help.

The types of reasoning and key questions are:

Cause-and-effect—"Is there a reasonable connection between cause and effect?"
    —"Are there other possible causes for this effect?"
Comparison—"How are the two cases similar and different?"
Generalization—"How large and representative is the sample?"

---

1. Eight out of 10 men who have a 38-inch waist and a 34-inch arm length have a particular shoulder size and pants length. So most of our uniforms can be of standard sizes, which will save us money.

    a. Type of reasoning:

    b. Question to ask:

    c. Evaluation of this argument:

2. Andrew Carnegie benefited mankind in many ways. He was a philanthropist and he improved steel production.

    a. Type of reasoning:

    b. Question to ask:

    c. Evaluation of this argument:

3. The trusts (monopolies) were responsible for the evils of industrial America in the late 1800s.

    a. Type of reasoning:

[Continued on next page.]

[Continued from previous page.]

    b. Question to ask:

    c. Evaluation of this argument:

4.   The Federal Government granted loans or land to railroads in the West only when track was completed. As a result, railroads stressed rapid construction which was poorly done.

    a. Type of reasoning:

    b. Question to ask:

    c. Evaluation of this argument:

5.   Most of the great captains of industry used the technique of "watered stock" to steal money from investors. That is, the captains of industry would control a business and then push the price of the company's stock far above the value of the company and sell this "watered down" stock to people.

    a. Type of reasoning:

    b. Question to ask:

    c. Evaluation of this argument:

6.   America's GNP rose from $165 per person in 1869–73 to $231 per person in 1897–1901. So Americans were obviously better off financially.

    a. Type of reasoning:

    b. Question to ask:

    c. Evaluation of this argument:

LESSON 14   Should the Government Role Be Laissez-faire or the General Welfare State?

Background Information

After the Civil War, thinkers in the United States (and also in Europe) engaged in a great philosophical debate about the proper role of government in society. They argued about whether the government should help the poor, regulate business to protect workers and consumers, promote labor unions, run public education and post offices, control the money supply, keep high tariffs, and many other issues.

Some thinkers believed in a philosophy called "laissez-faire" which basically means hands off (literally "allow them to do"). They wanted the government to be reduced to the smallest size and fewest functions possible. They felt the proper role of government was to protect life and property. Nothing else. The government had no positive role in helping the general welfare.

The philosophy of laissez-faire came from a number of sources, two of which were classical economics and Darwinism. Classical economics is represented in the first viewpoint by Adam Smith. Classical economists were reacting against government interference in the economy under the philosophy of mercantilism. They felt government interference was inefficient and hurt economic growth. The second source of laissez-faire was derived from the views of Charles Darwin. In 1859 Darwin published *The Origin of Species* in which he argued that species had evolved, they were not created. Competition for survival in nature is fierce—only the fittest survive. The few that do survive and reproduce the next generation have been selected naturally. Thus the survivors of any species are changing over generations as they adapt to changes in the environment. It should be noted that Dar-

win never wrote that his theory of nature should apply also to society. The social Darwinist source of the laissez-faire philosophy is represented here most directly by Herbert Spencer and William Graham Sumner. Social Darwinists believed that government involvement in society interfered with the natural selection of those best suited to survival in society.

The philosophy of the general welfare state, called the Social Gospel, was partly a reaction by Christian thinkers in the United States. These thinkers, represented here by Washington Gladden, felt individualism had gone too far and needed to be balanced with Christian concern for one's neighbors. The general welfare state philosophy also was a reaction to rapid changes in society resulting from industrialization and urbanization. These thinkers felt the laissez-faire approach was not helping solve the problems arising from industrialization.

Each of the viewpoints that follow is a summary of what that thinker wrote. Some of these thinkers wrote thousands of pages, so remember that these viewpoints are very simplistic summaries of what they said. Read the viewpoints and fill in the sheet your teacher gives you. The first five thinkers (A-E) are in favor of laissez-faire while the second five (F-J) favor the general welfare state. They are arranged in the order in which they wrote.

Keep in mind that there are differences within each group of thinkers. Some believe the principles of laissez-faire or general welfare state should be applied in every case, while others allow for exceptions.

The question we want to answer is: "To

[Continued on next page.]

[Continued from previous page.]

what extent should the government interfere in society?" Proponents of pure laissez-faire say the government should stay out of society, while proponents of the general welfare state say the government has many legitimate roles in society.

Thinker A

Adam Smith (From *The Wealth of Nations*, 1776)

(1) Self-interest is what motivates people to do things. Each individual knows much better than the government what is best for himself. To further his economic self-interest each person sells his labor or produces goods that people want to buy. No one sells unless he feels he is getting the best (highest) price that he can get. No one buys unless he feels he is paying the lowest price under the circumstances. Therefore, every sale in the marketplace is a transaction in which both people feel they have increased their self-interest. (If they did not, they would not have bought or sold.) Thus, the sum total of all the millions of sales is that millions of people have benefited. In this way, by each person doing what he thinks is best in the marketplace for his own self-interest, the general welfare of all the people in society is improved.

(2) Moreover, the marketplace is extremely efficient, since it reacts immediately to changes in demand and supply. Government can never adapt fast enough to the millions of changes in the market which take place from day to day.

(3) The area of labor is also controlled by the market. An employer, to serve his self-interest, will try to hire as cheaply as possible. A laborer, to serve his self-interest, will attempt to get the highest wages he can. The price arrived at will be subject to the natural law of supply and demand. Unionization, a form of monopoly, only serves to interfere with the free operation of the market, which leads to labor shortages, inefficiencies, and poor work.

(4) When the marketplace is left uncontrolled to work according to the laws of supply and demand, everyone's economic freedom is assured since no one individual is in control of events. It is when the government interferes in the market that the economy becomes less efficient, freedom is restricted, and economic growth retarded.

Thinker B

Herbert Spencer (From *Social Statics*, 1851; *The Study of Sociology*, 1896; *The Principles of Ethics*, 1897; and other writings)

(1) Animals are in a constant struggle for survival. The fastest water buffalo survive while the slowest and weakest are killed first. In this way, nature weeds out the inferior members of each species and thereby constantly improves them.

(2) Just as in these lower creatures, humans also are involved in a struggle for existence. If the human species is to be preserved, it, like all other species, must permit benefits to flow to people according to their merit (that is, their ability to survive). If each person received the benefits or suffered the evil results of his own actions (the law of conduct and consequence) the individuals best adapted to their environment would prosper most, those least adapted would prosper least, and, as a result, the fittest would survive and human progress would be assured.

(3) On the other hand, any interfer-

[Continued on next page.]

Thinker B

[Continued from previous page.]

ence with the law of conduct and consequence only hurts the welfare of humans. Were the superior individual in any way made to assume the burdens of the inferior, the superior would be held back and the inferior, the good-for-nothings, would increase faster. Society would be populated by fewer people of merit and more inferior people. The natural process by which society continually purifies itself would be stopped.

(4) This law of conduct and consequence (leading to survival of the fittest), is closely associated with a second, the law of equal freedom. In this law, every man has freedom to do anything he wants, so long as he does not interfere with the freedom of any other man.

(5) It follows from these two laws that the government should limit itself to the administration of justice (for example, judging claims in court) and protecting citizens from crimes and invasion from other countries. Every other expansion of government is wrong. It limits people's freedom and interferes with survival of the fittest.

(6) Laws to help the poor, sanitation laws, public education, government-owned post offices, regulation of currency (money supply) and working conditions, public works, and tariffs are all examples of too much government, since they all go beyond the minimum role of government to provide justice and protect against invasion. Public education, for example, takes tax money from many people, thus limiting their freedom, and provides education free to the children of some people, thus relieving them of their parental responsibility to educate their own children.

(7) Legislators (lawmakers) do not realize that their laws always have unintended, negative long-term effects. Since society is so complex, there is no way to calculate these effects. Society changes very slowly according to a gigantic plan. The government official comes with his puny laws to put a patch upon nature. He dares to announce that he and his colleagues have found a way to improve upon the Divine plan.

(8) The history of mankind is the progression toward less government. As society develops a stronger moral sense, people operate more freely, and government has fewer functions. Thus does society advance.

Thinker C

William Graham Sumner (From Albert Galloway Keller and Maurice R. Davie, eds., *Essays of William Graham Sumner*, 1934. The essays were written in the late 1800s.)

(1) Societies are controlled by natural laws just as the universe is controlled by natural laws. All of mankind's social activity is determined (controlled) by the stage of industrial organization existing at the time. So, government interference cannot change the existing situation.

(2) What government does is harmful in other ways, however. It undermines the personal freedom of the individual. For, when government interferes in people's lives, it tells them what they can and cannot do. Government interference, such as factory laws (to improve working conditions) and child labor laws, is also wrong because it is against the laws of nature.

[Continued on next page.]

Thinker C

[Continued from previous page.]

(3) It is true that we have rich and poor in our society, but that is to be expected. The rich industrialists (owners of large industrial corporations) deserve to be rich as a reward for their work which brings about advance to society. On the other hand, the situation of the poor is mostly their own fault. The poor are poor because they are lazy. If every man were hard working and wise, and if he brought his children up to be the same way, poverty would be abolished (done away with) in a few generations. Everyone is entitled to a chance, but not to success.

(4) True, we as a society should take care of true paupers and the physically handicapped who need help. But the social reformers want to help the poor in general. Whatever money is used to support the shiftless and good-for-nothing person (which many of the poor are) cannot be used for whoever had the money before, likely a hard-working person. The poor are poor because they produce less than the middle class and wealthy. If poor people produced something useful for society, they would no longer be poor since society would pay them to get it. Thus, the poor are less productive than the rest of society.

If money is diverted (turned to a different use) by the government from the middle class and wealthy to the poor, it is really being diverted from the productive part of the economy to the unproductive part of the economy. As more money is put into the unproductive part of the economy, fewer goods are produced (since less money is in the part of the economy which produces goods). Thus, the next year the economy is not as big as it would have been if it had been left alone. Since there is more poverty resulting from this lack of growth, more money is spent to help the poor (i.e., diverted to the unproductive part of the economy). The net result after several years is that because of government aid to the poor everyone, including the poor, is worse off! The pie graphs below illustrate this argument. Obviously, the poor are better off with a same-size share of a larger economy, than a larger share of a progressively smaller economy.

(5) Human society is too complex for the human mind to understand, let alone change through reforms or government laws. Society is not something artificial

[Continued on next page.]

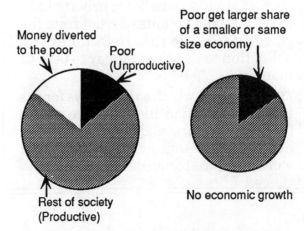

Without Government Aid to the Poor

YEAR 1   YEAR 2

Poor (Unproductive)

Poor get same percentage of wealth but of a larger economy

Rest of society (Productive)

Size of 1st year economy

Economic growth

With Government Aid to the Poor

YEAR 1   YEAR 2

Money diverted to the poor

Poor (Unproductive)

Poor get larger share of a smaller or same size economy

Rest of society (Productive)

No economic growth

Thinker C

[Continued from previous page.]

that can be changed, it is an organism (a living thing) which changes despite our attempts at interference. When we try to get rid of one evil, we cause another.

(6) Moreover, history demonstrates that ambitious persons have always tried to gain control of the government so as to live off the earnings of other persons. Reformers pass laws and set up agencies to help the public, but the rich people end up controlling the agencies. The main person who ends up paying for all these schemes is the "forgotten man." He is the average tax-paying middle-class citizen who is honest and independent and who asks no favors for himself. We must reduce the government to prevent the rich from using their economic power to gain political power also, and to allow the "forgotten man" his freedom to produce goods that end up benefiting society.

(7) The evidence is that the poor like their life, because it satisfies their strongest desires. They should not get help from society. By letting them alone, we cure the problems of poverty, crime, and filth by nature's method—we allow many of the poor to die in the struggle of the survival of the fittest. In this way society cleans out the less fit.

(8) There are only two choices: liberty, inequality, survival of the fittest; or not-liberty, equality, survival of the unfittest. The first way makes for civilization and progress, the second way brings anticivilization and retrogression (going backwards).

Thinker D

Andrew Carnegie (From *The Gospel of Wealth*, 1900; and other writings)

(1) Freedom is the right of each person to gain as much wealth as he can through hard work and thrift. Equality is equal opportunity for financial wealth, not welfare by the government taken from the rich through taxes and given to the poor. Progress does not come from the government but from the ever-increasing production of industries.

(2) If there is to be any charity for the poor, it should come from private individuals giving voluntarily, not from the government. The rich, in fact, have an obligation to use their money to benefit mankind.

(3) The price which society pays for the law of competition, like the price it pays for cheap comforts and luxuries, is great, but the advantages of this law is our wonderful material development and improved conditions. There is no substitute for the law of competition, and while the law may be sometimes hard for the individual, it is best for the race, because it insures the survival of the fittest. We accept and welcome, therefore, great inequality, the concentration of business in the hands of a few, and the law of competition between these few, as being beneficial and essential for the future progress of the race.

(4) Since each individual in his pursuit of wealth unconsciously promotes the general good, those who are most successful in getting wealth (millionaires) are the most successful in promoting the general good. The millionaires are the bees that make the most honey, and contribute most to the hive, even after they have gorged themselves full. Since they contribute the most to the economy, the successful businessmen deserve the largest share of what is produced.

[Continued on next page.]

Thinker E

Horatio Alger (Alger wrote children's fiction books, such as *Ragged Dick*, 1867. His ideas are inferred from the stories in the books.)

(1) People rise from poverty by working hard, being thrifty, and seizing "the main chance." When people do some good deed, they are rewarded with good luck.

(2) The capitalist system rewards people who have ability and work hard by allowing them the freedom to gain riches. Such a system which provides an opportunity to everyone for getting wealth should not be interfered with by government.

Thinker F

Henry George (From *Progress and Poverty*, 1879)

(1) Why is it that in America we have the "House of Have" (great wealth) and the "House of Want" (great poverty) standing side by side? It is from the unearned increase in the value of land which the rich get, since all economic advances come from the productive use of land. For example, the value of land would go up if a railroad was built through an area. But a report of the coming railroad would send land speculators rushing in to buy up the available land. The value of the land would multiply several times over. The speculators would then charge rent to the rest of the population. Notice that the speculators did nothing to improve the land, but they made all the profit. Meanwhile, the people who labored to improve the land, the workers on the railroad, received none of the profit. In fact, the workers got charged more rent for the land they improved.

(2) It is certainly a terrible situation which creates progress for the useless landlord and poverty for the useful worker. From this basic injustice flow all the injustices in our society, which condemn the producer of wealth to poverty and give the nonproducer wealth and luxury.

(3) To solve this problem, the government should tax the unearned growth in land values and should use the money to help the rest of society.

Thinker G

Richard T. Ely (From *The Labor Movement in America*, 1886; *Studies in the Evolution of Industrial Society*, 1909; and other writings)

(1) There are a number of flaws in the thinking of those, such as Adam Smith, who support the philosophy of laissez-faire. First, they base their theory on general economic laws which never change. But as Darwin has shown, all life changes, so economic theories are just an outgrowth of the economic conditions of the time. Economic theories must, of necessity, change. A look at economic information shows that classical, laissez-faire economics arose in a preindustrial society in reaction to mercantilism. Today (1880s), however, we live in a much more complex industrial society—too complex for the simple models of the classical economists.

(2) The classical economists say that man is motivated by self-interest and self-interest brings about general benefit for society. But man is obviously motivated by reasons other than self-interest, such as devotion to principle and a sense of helping one's fellow man. Also, the interests of the individual and

[Continued on next page.]

Thinker G

[Continued from previous page.]

the interests of society are not identical as shown by the destruction of the countryside to get resources. Private self-interest is too immoral and too shortsighted to promote the public good.

(3) Proponents of laissez-faire say the government is too inefficient and corrupt to accomplish anything worthwhile in society. The governments are not effective, however, precisely because the laissez-faire philosophy keeps them restricted. This weakness in government has persuaded men of talent to offer their services to private companies. Also, weak government is easy prey for powerful corporations. If the government were given more important duties, men of talent would be attracted to public service; the government would become more efficient; and it would be better able to resist the corrupting influence of special interests (for example, lobbyists for the railroads).

(4) The laissez-faire society stresses the negative aspects of liberty (let people do what they want without regulation). But under laissez-faire everyone's liberty is reduced. There are greater inequalities in wealth, abuse of the weak by the strong, and little opportunity for many people. By stressing regulation in the name of the public interest, government could bring about more opportunity for the bulk of the population and thus enhance liberty.

(5) While competition is a necessary part of our economy, industrialization brings a great deal of unequal competition. For example, unorganized workers cannot compete on an equal basis with industrial employers (owners) who can fix wages at a very low level. Workers have the right to organize into unions to make the competition more equal. Government must protect that right.

(6) Some social Darwinists feel that individualism is a great ideal of Christianity and that competition is morally right. But extreme individualism is morally wrong—it leads to the breakdown of society. Cain (from Cain and Abel in the Bible) was the first extreme individualist when he asked if he were his brother's keeper. Laissez-faire policies assure us that we are not keepers of our brothers, that each one best promotes (advances) the general interest of society by promoting his own. Actually, the main way to protect the public interest and insure fair competition is through government involvement in the economy.

(7) Man is much more than an economic decision-maker. He is involved in many relationships and is motivated by political, social, psychological, religious, and ethical reasons. Economics should be subjected to ethical principles. What good is economic production if it does not benefit the people in society? The individual is not a mere pawn of the environment, under the control of natural laws. Rather, man achieves progress by subjugating (controlling) nature. Within certain limits we can have the kind of economic life we wish by taking control, by using the government of all the people to accomplish our goals.

[Continued on next page.]

[Continued from previous page.]

Thinker H

Washington Gladden (From *Social Facts and Forces*, 1897)

(1) Industrial conditions today are deplorable. If men only followed the true teachings of Jesus (such as loving your neighbor as yourself) the conditions in our society would be greatly improved.

(2) The present laissez-faire system stresses selfishness and competition which is thoroughly unchristian. A Christian society, which we call ourselves, must be organized on the basis of cooperation rather than competition.

(3) The proponents of laissez-faire say labor is a commodity, like steel, and the wages for workers is to be determined by the impersonal forces of supply and demand. In reality, the laboring man is a human being—he is not to be measured in terms of dollars and cents. The employer must remember in dealing with his employees that he is dealing not with merchandise from which he is to make a profit, but with children of God, whose welfare must be his constant concern.

(4) Corporations, left to themselves, lower the morality of our country. For example, suppose four businessmen were competing in an industry, and three of the businessmen were honest and one was immoral. If the immoral owner could lower his prices by doing something immoral, then he could undersell his three competitors and take over the industry. The three other businessmen now face a dilemma. If they remain honest, the immoral businessman will eventually run the whole industry. Or the three businessmen can become dishonest to compete effectively with the immoral owner. In this case, four immoral businessmen will run the industry.

(5) Since business moves naturally toward lower standards of morality, we need government regulation to insure equal and fair competition and promote higher standards of morality for our society.

Thinker I

Lester Frank Ward (From *Glimpses of the Cosmos*, 1913)

(1) Almost everything we enjoy today, from good food to good health, comes from scientific investigation. It is man's intelligence, his ability to plan and order the universe, which separates him from animals. For the government to get involved and order things is just being intelligent.

(2) There is no need for mankind to continue to be crushed by natural laws and play the deadly game of survival of the fittest. People who favor social Darwinism and the laissez-faire doctrine say that the government should not intervene in the natural flow of events—that we should not interfere with natural laws. But these people forget that all human development is the result of just such interference. The inventor, who the laissez-faire supporters feel is so good and who should be left alone by the government, is a meddler in the natural course of development. If our society never interfered with natural laws our society would fall apart. Government meddlers, like scientific meddlers, help improve society.

(3) The supporters of laissez-faire say that government is inefficient. But it is

[Continued on next page.]

Thinker I

[Continued from previous page.]

inefficient because it is not yet based on scientific principles. The general public must be educated in scientific education, especially sociology. Government officials should be trained in the science and art of government. Then we would gather statistics and plan for sound operation of the national economy. Attractive legislation, such as subsidies to certain economic activities would divert human desires and resources into socially useful channels.

(4) Another weakness of the government is that the rich, through the philosophy of laissez-faire, make the general public view the government as a threat rather than a help to society. The rich industrialists say the state should not interfere in the economy, but they want to keep their own government help, such as tariffs and legalization of trusts (monopolies). The government which does not protect the weak, is protecting the strong.

(5) If we continue to have the rich, unhindered by any regulations to fulfill their obligations to society, get richer while the poor and powerless continue to get poorer, then we will have revolution. Wealth is a trust of society—no one could pile up wealth without other people to provide services, to provide labor, and to buy the products. Thus, society has a right to regulate what happens to that wealth. In so doing, the government can bring about a more equal distribution of wealth between rich and poor, and thereby avoid revolution.

Thinker J

Thorstein Veblen (From *The Theory of Business Enterprise*, 1904)

(1) The very rich investors in America are neither useful to society, nor the product of the "survival of the fittest." They are actually vultures who live off industries by piling up wealth through finance (investing money or banking). For example, Jay Gould made a great deal of money by destroying the Erie Railroad. He made all his profits by selling stocks in the railroads, not by making improvements in it. The Erie Railroad should have been run by engineers, who would have taken pride in running it well.

(2) The industrious people (workers, engineers) make goods by their work and by building upon previous knowledge of how to make goods. The improvement of industry benefits society. But the business class, the investors, make all the profit by controlling the funds necessary for industry to really help society. Businessmen make no contribution to material progress; they just live off the industrious.

(3) Making money through profits is supposed to be a reward for helping society by making something useful. In our society making money is the end itself. There is no necessary benefit to society.

(4) America should not run according to the laissez-faire doctrine in which we sit back and allow the rich to manipulate the economy to plunder (steal from) the rest of society.

[Continued on next page.]

[Continued from previous page.]

 The Ten Thinkers

Thinker A—Adam Smith

1. How does the market convert self-interest into the general good?

2. Why is the marketplace more efficient than government?

3. Evaluate the reasoning used in the first paragraph. What possible fallacy is Smith committing? (See pp. 10–11 in the "Guide to Critical Thinking.")

Thinker B—Herbert Spencer

4. Identify and evaluate the type of reasoning used in the first sentence of the second paragraph.

[Continued on next page.]

[Continued from previous page.]

5. What assumption does Spencer make about rich and poor people?

6. What is wrong with government programs to help the general population?

Thinker C—William Graham Sumner

7. Why do the rich deserve to be rich and the poor to be poor?

8. Why is government help for poor people a bad idea?

9. Who gets hurt by government interference?

[Continued on next page.]

[Continued from previous page.]
Thinker D—Andrew Carnegie

10. Evaluate the argument in the first sentence of paragraph 4.

Thinker E—Horatio Alger

11. Do poor people deserve to be poor, according to Alger?

Thinker F—Henry George

12. How do the rich get their money? Do they deserve it?

Thinker G—Richard T. Ely

13. What are three weaknesses of the laissez-faire philosophy stressed in paragraphs 1 and 2?

[Continued on next page.]

[Continued from previous page.]

14. According to Ely, what is wrong with laissez-faire on the following?

   a. Government (paragraphs 3 and 4)

   b. Workers' wages (paragraph 5)

   c. Individualism (paragraph 6)

Thinker H—Washington Gladden

15. What's wrong with treating labor (workers) as a commodity to be bought and sold like any other product?

16. What happens to the level of morality of corporations if unchecked by government regulation? (paragraph 4)

[Continued on next page.]

[Continued from previous page.]

Thinker I—Lester Frank Ward

17. What's wrong with the laissez-faire philosophy about men and government interference in nature? (paragraphs 1 and 2)

18. Why is the government in the state it is in? (paragraphs 3–5)

19. Evaluate the argument in paragraph 4.

Thinker J—Thorstein Veblen

20. How do the rich businessmen make their money and how does it affect society?

21. Evaluate Veblen's view of rich businessmen (investors).

[Continued on next page.]

[Continued from previous page.]

 Fill in the worksheet on the next page (p. 89) by listing two or three of the best arguments of each thinker in preparation for a debate on the proposition:

> To what extent should government interfere in society?

 After completing the worksheet, decide which position, laissez-faire or general welfare state, you favor. Or are you undecided? Explain which position you prefer in the space below (even for undecided).

[Continued on next page.]

Arguments for and against Laissez-faire

THINKER	List 2 or 3 (as indicated) of each thinker's best arguments in your own words. Star the best argument.
A. Smith	1 2 3
B. Spencer	1 2 3
C. Sumner	1 2 3
D. Carnegie	1 2
E. Alger	1 2
F. George	1 2
G. Ely	1 2 3
H. Gladden	1 2 3
I. Ward	1 2 3
J. Veblen	1 2

LAISSEZ-FAIRE SURVEY

	STATEMENT	AGREE / DISAGREE— EXPLAIN YOUR ANSWER
1.	The people who work the hardest usually get ahead, and this means society is constantly getting better.	
2.	If we help the poor, then we are all worse off.	
3.	If we help the poor, then the poor will become lazy.	
4.	It's hard to survive in this world, so only the fittest stay alive (survival of the fittest).	
5.	All animals, including man, produce more children than can survive.	
6.	The free market (capitalist) system gives all people a chance for success.	
7.	More equality is more important than more freedom.	
8.	Economic growth comes from hardworking people.	

LESSON 15   What is Significant about the Life of John D. Rockefeller?

The information below is about John D. Rockefeller. Use it to write a maximum 300-word biography of Rockefeller. In your biography show what kind of person he was and what was significant about him. What does his life show about American society during his time? You do not have to use all the information below. Just select the information which will help you write the biography.

1. John D. Rockefeller was worth over $1 billion dollars by 1910, making him by far the richest man in America.

2. Rockefeller believed in "tithing," that is, contributing 10% of his income to the church. In 1905 he contributed $100 million to the Baptist Church.

3. There was no income tax in the United States until 1913.

4. In 1905 the Congregational Missions Board rejected a Rockefeller gift of $100,000 because it was "tainted money." They felt the money had been earned in an unethical way through the Standard Oil Company.

5. Rockefeller always said he was a decent man who earned his money fairly. Jay Gould and other robber barons bragged about how they had cheated to get their money. Rockefeller said he was a Christian businessman.

6. Senator La Follette called Rockefeller the "greatest criminal of the age."

7. Washington Gladden, a protestant minister, commented on a Rockefeller contribution to the church, "Is this clean money? On every side wealth had been accumulated by methods as heartless, as cynically iniquitous as any employed by the Roman plunderers or robber barons of the dark ages. In the cool brutality with which properties are wrecked, securities destroyed, and people by the hundreds robbed of their little, all to build up the fortunes of the millionaires, we have an appalling revelation of the kind of monster that a human being may become."

8. John D. Rockefeller said he grew up in a poor family. His sister said that was nonsense. "We weren't rich," she said, "but we had enough."

9. John's father was William Avery Rockefeller, known as "Doc" Rockefeller. "Doc" went to religious camp meetings and sold patent medicines—he was a con artist. His handbills stated: "Dr. Wm. A. Rockefeller, the celebrated cancer specialist, here for one day only. All cases of cancer cured unless too far gone, and even then they can be greatly benefited." Rockefeller charged $25 for consultations, almost 2 months wages.

10. "Doc" Rockefeller was indicted (charged) for raping a female worker who worked for the family.

11. "Doc" Rockefeller was rarely home. John found out later that his father had been secretly married to another woman in South Dakota for 40 years.

[Continued on next page.]

[Continued from previous page.]

12. Mr. Dooley, a humorous newspaper writer said, "John D. Rockefeller is a kind of society for the prevention of cruelty to money. If he finds a man misusing his money, he takes it away from him and adopts it."

13. Rockefeller was not disliked for piracy, but rather for the tremendous wealth and power he had. He was undemocratic with all that wealth and power.

14. John learned from his father that impulsiveness was dangerous. As an adult he told some children, "Sixty years ago my father promised me a Shetland pony—I never got it."

15. Rockefeller's mother, Eliza, was thin, stark and thrifty. She was a Calvinist and read the Bible at night. She was rational, unlike her impulsive husband who humiliated and abandoned her.

16. Rockefeller's mother believed that "willful waste makes woeful want." One time she was switching (spanking with a stick) John when she learned he had not committed the offense. She finished switching him stating, "It will do for next time."

17. John was small and weak as a child.

18. The Rockefeller family moved to Cleveland when John was 14. He had few friends at Cleveland Central High School, where his over-serious attitude won him the nickname "the deacon."

19. Some boyhood incidents and quotes:

    • When John was 7 years old he took a wild turkey from its mother and sold it for a profit.

    • He saved $50 in three years and loaned it to a farmer at 7% interest. The interest was more than for 10 days work, working 10 hours per day hoeing potatoes. Rockefeller said, "From that time on I determined to make money work for me."

    • John's sister said, "When it is raining porridge, you'll always find John's bowl right side up."

    • John said to a friend, "I want to be worth $100,000 and I'm going to be, too."

20. On September 26, 1855, John was hired by Hewett and Tuttle (grain shippers) as a clerk accountant (keeping financial records).

21. He taught Sunday School at Erie Street Baptist Church in Cleveland.

    • His favorite text was: "Seest thou a man diligent in his business. He will stand before kings."

    • Other favorite sayings: "Pride goeth before the fall." "Nothing in haste, nothing ill done."

22. The only surviving written record from his childhood was "Ledger A." It kept track of all income and expenses. No other notes or entries were kept in it.

[Continued on next page.]

[Continued from previous page.]

23. He and a man named M.B. Clark formed a company called Clark and Rockefeller in 1858. The company made $4000 profit the first year and $17,000 profit the second year.

24. John borrowed $1000 from his father at 10% interest. His father said, "I cheat my boys every chance I get. I skin 'em every time I can. I want to make them sharp." John did not like his father's attitude of trying to cheat and test him.

25. John did not serve in the army during the Civil War. He said, "I wanted to go into the army and do my part, but it was simply out of the question. There was no one else who could take my place. We were in a new business, and if I had not stayed, it must [would] have stopped."

26. The oil business grew rapidly after Drake struck oil at Titusville, Pennsylvania in 1859. A railroad connection in 1863 from the oil region to Cleveland caused the growth of many oil refineries in Cleveland.

27. Rockefeller invested as a partner in Andrews and Clark Oil Refinery. John focused on details and cutting waste. He had the company make its own barrels and buy its own wagons to cut costs. He drove the hardest bargain possible. A man who worked with him said, "The only time I saw John Rockefeller enthusiastic was when a report came from the creek [oil creek] that his buyer had secured a cargo of oil much below the market price. He bounded from his chair with a shout of joy, danced up and down, hugged me, [and] threw up his hat."

28. In 1864 John married Laura (Settie) Spelman. Her parents were involved in their Christian church, helping blacks, and the temperance movement. John's written record of the wedding was: "September 8, 1864: Married at 2 o'clock p.m. to Miss L.C. Spelman by Rev. D. Wolcott assisted by Rev. Page at the residence of her parents."

29. In early 1865 John bought out Clark from the oil refining firm for $72,500. John said, "[It was] one of the most important [days] of my life." He was 26 years old.

30. There was an oil boom from the Civil War. Rockefeller correctly expanded. His company was the largest oil refinery in Cleveland in 1865, twice the size of the next largest refinery. He said, "I'm bound to be rich!"

31. His company leased all the oil tank cars so other refiners could not get them. The company also got rebates (secret refunds) from the railroads.

32. In 1870 the Standard Oil Company was formed, run mainly by Rockefeller. Later that year Standard Oil joined the South Improvement Company (SIC). The oil companies in the SIC got rebates from the railroads which gave them a big advantage over other oil companies. The SIC also gave stock in the company to bankers in Cleveland so the banks would not make loans to other oil companies.

33. John wrote to his brother about the South Improvement Company, "We have a combination [an agreement to form one business out of several] with the railroads. We're going to buy out all the refiners in Cleveland. We will give everyone a chance to come in. Those who refuse will be crushed. If they don't sell their property to us it will be valueless."

BIOGRAPHY WORKSHEET

A biography is supposed to tell the reader what a person is like: what is important to them; the kind of personality they have (shy, sensitive, loudmouthed, kind, go-getter, smart, competitive, outgoing, money worshiper, etc.); what influenced them to become the way they are (childhood, friends, religion, school); their greatest accomplishments or failures; what they show about the society of their time.

 To prepare for your biography of John D. Rockefeller, first you are going to interview another student and give an oral biography of that student.

- Step 1

  Make a list of questions to ask in the interview. For example, you might want to ask, "What do you do with your free time?" to find out something about the person's values.

- Step 2

  Choose the 5–10 questions that you think would be best to ask.

- Step 3

  Interview another student and write notes on the answers.

- Step 4

  Prepare for your oral biography of the other student by organizing your notes on another sheet of paper. In your oral biography be sure to include answers to these questions:

  1. What is the student's personality?

  2. What are the student's values or goals?

  3. What experiences helped shape the student's personality?

  4. What does this student show about our society?

- Step 5

  Give the oral biography of the student.

 Now read the information on John D. Rockefeller on pages 91–93. Take notes in answer to the following four questions, then write a maximum 300-word biography of Rockefeller.

  5. What was Rockefeller like? What was his personality?

  6. What were Rockefeller's goals? What did he value?

  7. How did Rockefeller get the way he was?

  8. What does Rockefeller show about American society in the late 1800s?

LESSON 16 Introduction to the Oil Business

Background Information

Beginning in the 1860s the demand for oil, or petroleum, increased dramatically. Most of the oil at the time came from oil wells in northwestern Pennsylvania in an area which came to be known as the oil region. (See the map below.) Most uses for oil required that it be refined. In the 1860s and 1870s the main use of oil was for kerosene used in lamps. Kerosene was refined from oil.

Due primarily to the Lake Shore Railroad, Cleveland became one of the centers of oil refining. Crude (unrefined) oil had to be transported up to 10 miles from the wells to the railroads, then shipped by railroad to the refineries. The refined oil was shipped again by railroad to market.

(Pipelines were eventually built to transport oil, but pipelines won't be dealt with in this lesson.) It is easy to see how important railroads were to the oil business. Changes in shipping rates could kill oil refineries. In fact, refineries worked on very small profit margins. Four cents per gallon was considered a high profit, and many refiners shipped thousands of barrels of oil per day (42 gallons in a barrel).

There were four major groups involved in the oil business: producers (drillers), railroads (shippers), refiners, and consumers of oil products. In this lesson you will read two viewpoints about a refining company, the Standard Oil Company, and its main owner, John D. Rockefeller.

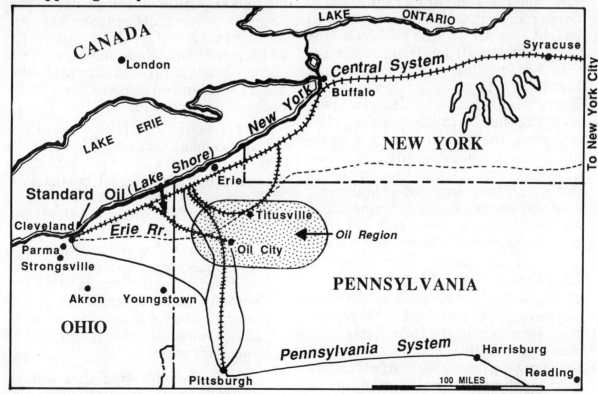

The Lake Shore Railroad was part of the New York Central System. Note that several railroads passed through Cleveland, giving refiners there a competitive advantage in shipping rates.

[Continued on next page.]

[Continued from previous page.]

Historian A (1904)

(1) This "History of the Standard Oil Company" is an outgrowth of an effort by McClure's magazine to inform its readers of the process by which a particular industry passes from the control of the many to the control of the few. The Standard Oil Company is an ideal business to study to show the growth of a monopoly. Many of the statements quoted in this study were given under oath which makes them more cautious and exact than the writings of memoirs. Standard Oil also gave me access to company records. All these statements and records give a clear picture of the growth of this monopoly.

(2) In the 1860s the demand for oil grew tremendously. In the oil region of Pennsylvania (see the map) supply surged also. The result was price fluctuations (rises and drops) which led to fierce competition. The shipment of oil freight was unfair. The open rate (the price advertised) for freight was enforced only on the people who did not know any better or on weak companies. Everyone else got secret deals for lower shipping charges (called rebates). Nevertheless, the businessmen and workers in the oil regions were decent people. They built towns, schools, operas and so forth; and they dreamed of building a civilized society in the oil region. But suddenly, at the very heyday of their confidence, a big hand reached out and throttled their future. That hand was from the Standard Oil Company.

(3) John D. Rockefeller was the moving force in the Standard Oil Company from its beginning in 1870. Rockefeller was a good businessman. He was great at borrowing money for business expansion. He eliminated waste and disorder, and he cut out the middleman wherever possible, saving the company money. And Rockefeller was tough at bargaining. The old men in Cleveland said, "John always got the best of the bargain."

(4) These business qualities were great, but they were not the main reason for Standard Oil's success. The key to the company's dominance over the oil industry was the secret rebate (lower railroad shipping rates). Railroads are public carriers so they have no right to give special rates to certain people. They must offer equal access to all customers. Rockefeller made his millions basically by using an unfair advantage over his competitors. Nowhere is this more apparent than in the South Improvement Company.

(5) Set up in 1872, the South Improvement Company was a conspiracy to buy up or drive out all the oil refineries in Cleveland. The railroads gave Standard Oil and any other oil companies in the South Improvement Company huge rebates in exchange for regular shipments on their railroads. Rockefeller used this shipping advantage to threaten the other Cleveland oil refiners. He went to each refiner and said:

> This scheme [the South Improvement Company] is bound to work. It means an absolute control by us of the oil business. There is no chance for anyone outside. But we are going to give everybody a chance to come in [to the company]. You are to turn over your refinery to my appraisers, and I will give you Standard Oil Company stock or cash, as you prefer, for the value we put upon it. I advise you to take the stock. It will be good for you.[1]

(6) Mr. Rockefeller said that selling out would be good for the other refiners. Actually, however, he was getting con-

[Continued on next page.]

Historian A

[Continued from previous page.]

trol of the other businesses for a fraction of their actual price. For example, Mr. Alexander was paid $65,000 for his company valued by Mr. Alexander at $150,000.[2] Of 26 refiners in Cleveland, 21 sold out. In three months the capacity of Standard Oil went from 1,500 to 10,000 barrels of oil per day, which was 20% of all the oil refined in the United States. Rockefeller had used a secret conspiracy and an unfair advantage to intimidate other oil refiners and become a dominant force in the industry.

(7) The oil producers and refiners in areas outside Cleveland joined together to stop the South Improvement Company. The general public also opposed the conspiracy, since one of the main purposes of the company was to keep the price of oil high at the expense of consumers. The public also realized that if a few refiners and railroads could throttle oil, they could throttle other products as well.[3] The opposition forced the railroads to give in and stop the rebate scheme. The South Improvement Company collapsed. On May 7, 1872, a month after the collapse, the Congressional Committee on Commerce made its report. It denounced the South Improvement Company as "one of the most gigantic and dangerous conspiracies ever attempted."

(8) Mr. Rockefeller was undaunted. In 1874 he introduced another scheme for control of oil refining. He told the other refiners present, "Let us unite secretly to become the nucleus of a private company which gradually shall acquire control of all refineries everywhere, become the only shippers, and consequently the master of the railroads in the matter of freight rates." Some independent refiners refused to sell out, placing their love of independent work above love for profits. Rockefeller could

not understand this willfulness. In these cases Standard Oil undersold the company, or threatened its suppliers or customers not to do business with it, until the company went out of business. For example, Standard Oil got control of all the railroad cars for shipping oil and prevented independent refiners from getting the cars.

(9) Rockefeller also wanted to keep the price of crude oil (which he bought to refine) as low as possible. If he bought crude oil at very low prices, paid low shipping rates, and sold the refined oil at much higher prices Rockefeller would make huge profits. As one crude oil company owner put it, "[The Standard Oil Company], by virtue of its monopoly of the business of refining and transportation of oil, had been at times almost the only buyers in the market, and at such times had been enabled to dictate a price for crude oil far below its actual value…and thus obtained a large share of the profits which should have fallen to the [oil producers]."

(10) Standard Oil got inside information on other oil refiners through bribing the companies' employees. For example, the bookkeeper of the Cleveland oil refinery of John Teagle was offered twenty-five dollars down and a small sum of money per year to copy Mr. Teagle's daily shipments, including amount, price, destination, and so forth. (Standard Oil executives said getting information about competitors was not company policy, that it was individuals from the company acting on their own trying to get the information. There were so many cases of such action, however, that it must have been company policy.)[4] Of course, Standard Oil used the information to threaten ship-

[Continued on next page.]

Historian A

[Continued from previous page.]

pers ("If you ship company X's oil, we'll hurt your company") and to crush other refiners.[5]

(11) Through these unfair advantages and cutthroat competition the Standard Oil Company eventually controlled over 90% of the oil refining in the United States. The industry had been transformed from competition to monopoly by the overarching will of one man.

(12) John D. Rockefeller was a "good" man in many ways. He was a faithful Baptist, gave liberally to the church, and gave to the poor and other charities. He did not drink wine and was simple and frugal in his habits. He was a devoted father and a good businessman. Yet he did everything he could to obtain special and unjust privileges from the railroads which were bound to ruin every man in the oil business not sharing in those privileges. He seemed to have no sense of justice or regard for the rights of others. When he was investigated he even lied on the witness stand.[6]

(13) Some people have argued that without Rockefeller the oil industry would have failed for lack of brains and capital (money and machinery). This argument is ridiculous. Oil was in great demand and greatly capitalized before Standard Oil began. Further, Standard Oil did not bring lower prices. If there were no Standard Oil the prices would have been even lower.

(14) As has been shown, Rockefeller used unethical practices in his business. It is clear that these actions were not taken to save his business, but rather, to destroy other businesses and build a monopoly. It is unfortunate that someone with such low ethical standards as John D. Rockefeller has been made into a business hero.

Endnotes for Historian A

[1] Numerous owners of oil refineries who did sell out testified that Rockefeller had made this argument. Mr. Rockefeller's own brother, Frank, also testified that John had intimidated the other refiners. "The Cleveland [oil refining] companies were told that if they didn't sell their property to them it would be valueless...."

[2] Testimony by Mr. Alexander to a Congressional Committee investigating the South Improvement Company.

[3] Article in the *New York Tribune.*

[4] John Teagle, testimony to a Congressional Committee, 1888. Teagle further said that the person from the Standard Oil company admitted that he had bribed the bookkeeper. An oil refiner in Marietta, Ohio told an Ohio Senate Committee in 1898 that a railroad agent in town had been asked by a Standard Oil representative for a full report on all independent shipments. A black boy was bribed by Standard Oil in 1893 to give information on the Lewis Emery Company of Philadelphia. The boy was caught and lost his job. Standard Oil even had regular forms for writing in the information on other companies, which certainly shows it was company policy.

[5] Statements by businessmen in Texas about the Waters-Pierce Oil Company, Standard Oil's agent (seller) in the state, give some information on their tactics to crush competitors:

"The Waters-Pierce Oil Company reduced their prices on Brilliant oil from $2.60 to $1.50 per case and is waging a fierce war."

"The day your oil arrived here, their agent [for Waters-Pierce] went to all my customers and offered their Eupion oil at ten cents per gallon in barrels and $1.50 per case, and lower grades in proportion, and told them if they did not refuse to take the oil [from the other company] he would not sell them any more [Waters-Pierce oil] at any price, and that he was going to run me out of business, and then they would be at his mercy."

[Continued on next page.]

Endnotes for Historian A
[Continued from previous page.]

"Now we think Waters-Pierce Oil Company have been getting too high a price for their oil. They are able and do furnish almost the entire state with oil. They cut prices to such an extent when any other oil is offered in this state that they force the parties handling the oil to abandon the trade."

[6] Rockefeller being questioned by a committee investigating monopolies in New York City in 1888:

Q—There was such a company? [As the South Improvement Company]

A—(Rockefeller) I have heard of such a company.

Q—Were you not in it?

A—I was not.

(Rockefeller owned 180 shares of the South Improvement Company.) Rockefeller was asked if Standard Oil received any cheaper rates than were allowed to the general public (rebates). Mr. Rockefeller answered: "No, sir." Contracts and agreements of rebates are in the records of the Standard Oil Company.

Historian B (1953)

(1) John D. Rockefeller and his Standard Oil Company have been a favorite target of critics over the years. Some of the criticism is justified. Rockefeller sometimes used ruthless tactics against competitors and the Standard Oil monopoly was clearly a threat to a free market economy. Nevertheless, the critics go too far in exaggerating Rockefeller's mistakes and in ignoring his accomplishments.

(2) In 1859, when Colonel Drake struck oil in western Pennsylvania, about 2000 barrels of oil were produced in the United States. Ten years later, in 1869, over 4 million barrels were produced. Although demand for oil increased rapidly it did not keep pace with this spectacular increase in supply. With supply outrunning demand, oil prices declined. From 1865 to 1870 oil refiners were squeezed by these falling prices and many went bankrupt.[1]

(3) Despite these difficulties in the oil industry, John D. Rockefeller built up the Standard Oil Company (formed in 1870) into the largest oil refinery in Cleveland. Rockefeller's enemies focused only on his advantages in transportation costs as the source of his success. They claimed Standard Oil got rebates (secret money repaid on the oil it shipped on the railroads) which lowered its costs below that of other refiners. Standard Oil then used these lower costs to drive other refiners out of business and take them over.

(4) This view greatly distorts what really made Standard Oil so successful. Rockefeller and the other managers were simply better organizers and used better business practices than their competitors. For example, they used careful bookkeeping; made their own oil barrels which were of better quality for half the cost; were the first to ship in their own tank cars and store oil in their own storage tanks; used better-planned factories; used the by-products of oil; borrowed as little as possible, which reduced interest costs; and reinvested heavily in plant (factory) improvements.

(5) Naturally, once the company grew it enjoyed the advantages of a large company. It could get crude oil for lower prices because of the large volume it bought. It could refine oil more cheaply because of its large factories and modern machinery. And it could command lower shipping rates from the railroads.

(6) The much criticized rebates the railroads offered to Standard Oil really

[Continued on next page.]

Historian B

[Continued from previous page.]

were not immoral—they made perfect economic sense. Actually, railroads offered rebates to shippers in many industries and they offered rebates to oil shippers long before Standard Oil was formed.[2] In addition, large shippers saved the railroads money so rebates were logical. Standard Oil pledged to ship 60 carloads of oil every day of the year on the Lake Shore Railroad. The railroad could therefore put together an all-oil train which would make only one stop, at its destination. This reduced the 30-day round trips for mixed trains making numerous stops to only 10 days. Maintenance, depreciation, payroll, and a host of other costs would be greatly reduced by the efficiency of such large and regular shipments. The railroad was obviously saving money.

(7) Rockefeller himself was dismayed by the outcry against rebates. He complained in 1917, "So much of the clamor against rebates and drawbacks came from people who knew nothing about business. Who can buy beef cheapest—the housewife for her family, the steward for a club or hotel, or the commissary for an army? These people would make no difference between wholesale and retail....Who is entitled to better rebates from a railroad, those who give it 5000 barrels a day, or those who give 500 barrels—or 50 barrels?"[3]

(8) Some people argue that railroads had no right to give rebates or secret deals to some shippers because the railroads were common carriers. That is, by serving the public in general, railroads were morally obliged not to discriminate against some shippers. A great deal of evidence shows, however, that the "common carrier" idea came later in American history. John T. Flynn stated, "This idea [common carrier] had practically no public support in the six-

ties. The roads [railroads] were in the possession of men who believed they had a right to run them to suit themselves."[4] Judged by the standards of his own times, Rockefeller's acceptance of rebates was certainly reasonable behavior.

(9) In 1872 several railroads approached Standard Oil with the idea of the infamous South Improvement Company. In the scheme Standard Oil and any other refineries which joined would get rebates and drawbacks (money paid to them secretly on oil shipped by their competitors!). In return, the railroads would get somewhat higher rates overall and large stable shipments to divide up among themselves without competition. Since oil producers were not included, they criticized the South Improvement Company as a monopoly. Interestingly, to fight it they formed a monopoly of their own, the Petroleum Producer's Union.

(10) Rockefeller later defended his decision to join the South Improvement Company. No large company, he said, could afford not to seek discounts (rebates) since his rivals would. Nevertheless, drawbacks were savage and indefensible. Rockefeller committed one of the great errors of his career when he joined the notorious scheme. The public viewed the South Improvement Company as a dangerous monopoly. Public opposition forced the collapse of the company after only a few months.

(11) Thus, the reckless competition among refiners, producers, and railroads continued unabated, and Rockefeller continued his dream of making the oil industry rational and profitable. In order to do this he had to limit competition. He decided to try to buy out the

[Continued on next page.]

Historian B

[Continued from previous page.]

other refiners in Cleveland. Later, some of these refiners claimed Rockefeller forced them to sell out at a fraction of their worth. Mr. Rockefeller tells a different story. He reminds us of the bad economic situation in 1872. "They didn't collapse [in the first three months of 1872]!" he cried. "They had collapsed before! That's the reason they were so glad to combine their interest with ours, or take the money we offered as an alternative." He stressed the ruinous competition before 1872 and denied he threatened anyone with the South Improvement Company. He added, "How could our company succeed if its members had been forced to join it and were working under the lash?"[5]

(12) Rockefeller recollects that he said to the other refiners, "We are here at a disadvantage. Something should be done for our mutual protection. We think it a good scheme [to sell out to Standard Oil]. Think it over. We would be glad to consider it with you if you are so inclined."[6] He offered to pay cash or Standard Oil stock (making them part of a profitable company).

(13) The charge that he forced rivals to sell at unfair prices angered Rockefeller. He pointed out that most of the companies had outdated equipment and that the companies themselves were unprofitable. Of what value was outdated equipment in a business which was overproducing? Thus, the price of equipment should not be valued at the original purchase price ($150,000 in the case of Mr. Alexander) but at its value in the market at the time ($65,000). In his later years, Rockefeller believed that Standard Oil had overvalued the property of the firms which sold out. "Much of it was old junk, fit only for the scrap heap." Standard Oil often did not even use the plants or equipment. Moreover,

Standard Oil stock always increased in value after the firms selling out took it. In Rockefeller's words, "The Standard was an angel of mercy, reaching down from the sky, and saying: 'Get into the ark. Put in your old junk. We'll take the risks!'"[7]

(14) Rockefeller's view of the buy-outs is supported by the only detailed record of negotiations between the Standard and an independent in 1872, made by Charles H. Tucker, secretary of Hanna, Baslington and Co., just before its purchase. In it no word of threat appears, and there is no complaint of unfair treatment by Mr. Hanna, the owner. Tucker complained later that their biggest mistake ("the mistake of our lives") was in taking cash instead of Standard Oil stock.[8] Tucker further said that the payment for the company was fair. Mr. Halle a partner in another company that sold out to Standard Oil shows payments were fair:

> "He [Rockefeller] treated everybody fairly. When we sold out he gave us a fair price. Some refiners tried to impose on him and when they could not do it they abused him. I remember one man whose refinery was worth $6000, or at most $8000. His friends told him, 'Mr. Rockefeller ought to give you $100,000 for that.' Of course, Mr. Rockefeller refused to pay more than the refinery was worth, and the man…abused Mr. Rockefeller."[9]

(15) After buying out the other Cleveland refiners, Standard Oil was the largest refiner in the United States. In the depression which began in 1873 more refiners sold out all over the country. Standard Oil acquired companies

[Continued on next page.]

Historian B

[Continued from previous page.]

in many cities, including New York, which increased its export business dramatically. As in Cleveland, refiners willingly sold out rather than face big losses.[10] In all these buy-outs Mr. Rockefeller was careful to keep the good men along with the new plants. Since Standard Oil had a reputation as an honest company, other companies trusted it and people tried hard to get employment in it.

(16) Thus the Standard Oil Company gained a virtual monopoly of oil refining in the United States. The story offers the picture of a vigorous, realistic, superbly-led organization, rising swiftly to a position of dominance over a new, ill-organized, chaotic industry. Standard Oil was ruthless, tyrannical, and deceptive at times, but the extreme disorganization of the oil industry in 1870 made heroic measures necessary to end its over production, price slashing, and competitive savagery, with their consequences of waste, bankruptcy, and suffering. Oil producers and railroads tried monopoly by pooling agreements—Standard Oil merely succeeded where others had failed.

(17) John D. Rockefeller was one of the most impressive American figures of the 19th and 20th centuries—foremost in business and in philanthropy. Rockefeller's greatness is shown in his character traits—his ambition, organizing power, insight, coolness under pressure, and ingenuity. Rockefeller's monopoly, like monopolies in so many industries at the time, was a natural response to unbridled competition. Judged against the moral standards of his day, Rockefeller did what he had to do to survive in a ruthless business environment. In the process of surviving and prospering, John D. Rockefeller brought stability, economy, and solvency to an important industry, and economic power to the country as a whole.

Endnotes for Historian B

[1]*Annual Reports*, Chamber of Commerce of the State of New York, 1865–71:

Year	Price of Crude Oil per gallon (the price oil refiners pay for oil to be refined)	Price of Refined Oil per gallon (the price oil refiners sell refined oil for)	Refiner's Margin of Profit
1865	38.37 cents	58.87 cents	19.50 cents
1866	25.78	42.45	16.67
1867	17.43	28.41	10.98
1868	19.66	29.52	9.86
1869	23.25	32.73	9.48
1870	18.45	26.35	7.90

[Continued on next page.]

Endnotes for Historian B
[Continued from previous page.]

2 *Report of the Railroad Commission, Ohio Senate Journal, 1867; Cleveland Leader*, February 4, 7, 25, 1867, contains the commission report and the bill proposed to the Ohio state house.

The Railroad Commission reported that rate reductions—rebates, drawbacks, special rates—were widespread in a variety of industries, especially coal. A bill to force companies to publish open rates without deviating from those rates was defeated in the Ohio state house. Note that the commission and the bill mentioned the rebates in 1867, before the formation of Standard Oil.

Henry Flagler, a Standard Oil official, stated, "Rebates and drawbacks were a common practice...for many years preceding and many years following this period; that is, the period before 1862 and long after."

3 W.O. Inglis, Notes of Conversations in the Moravia Neighborhood, July-August, 1917, in the Rockefeller papers. Conversations with John D. Rockefeller.

4 John T. Flynn, *God's Gold: The Story of Rockefeller and His Times.* (New York, 1932), p. 137.

5 Inglis, Conversations with Rockefeller, 1917.

6 Ibid.

7 Ibid.

8 W.O. Inglis, Conversation with Charles H. Tucker, 1917.

9 Inglis, Conversation with Mr. Halle, 1917.

10 The following conversation between William Harkness and his brother Norris about whether to sell their Philadelphia refinery to Standard Oil in 1876 was recorded in *House Trust Investigation, 1888*, p. 233ff.

Norris: "There is a good chance to get out. Warden, Frew and Company (Standard Oil Company) are willing to buy the plant for what we have put into it."

William: "Do you really think we had better sell? Or shall we fight it out?"

Norris: "I think we had better sell. We shall get our investment back. That is better than a heavy loss later on."

 ## Historian A

1. What is the main point of Historian A?

2. Evaluate the evidence by Rockefeller in endnote 1.

3. Evaluate the evidence in endnote 2.

[Continued on next page.]

[Continued from previous page.]

4. Evaluate the evidence in endnote 4.

5. Identify and evaluate the type of reasoning used in the last sentence in paragraph 6. You might want to make a diagram in your evaluation. Remember that you are to make a judgment (strong/weak) of the reasoning.

6. Identify and evaluate the type of reasoning used in the third sentence in paragraph 10 (the sentence in parentheses).

7. Identify one unstated assumption of Historian A. What is one thing he believes is true about life or business?

8. Identify one value of Historian A.

[Continued on next page.]

[Continued from previous page.]

 Historian B

9. What is the main point of Historian B?

10. Evaluate the evidence in endnote 2.

11. Evaluate the evidence in endnote 6.

12. Evaluate the evidence in endnote 8. (Consider endnote 9 in your evaluation.)

13. Identify and evaluate the reasoning used in paragraphs 4 and 5. Consider making a diagram.

[Continued on next page.]

[Continued from previous page.]

14. Identify and evaluate the reasoning used in paragraph 7.

15. Identify and evaluate the reasoning used in paragraph 13, sentence 2.

16. Identify and evaluate the reasoning used in paragraph 15, sentence 4 .

17. Identify one unstated assumption of Historian B. What is one thing he believes is true about life or business?

18. Identify one value of Historian B.

[Continued on next page.]

[Continued from previous page.]

 General Questions

19. List two points on which Historians A and B agree.

 1—

 2—

20. Look at the information in Lesson 15 (pp. 91–93) about John D. Rockefeller. How does this information affect your judgment of the two historical interpretations? In the space below, list two pieces of information, including the number of each, and explain whether the information strengthens or weakens one of the two viewpoints (A or B).

[Continued on next page.]

[Continued from previous page.]

Assumptions of Historians A and B

 On the line next to each statement write the letter of the historian you think would agree with it, as listed below. Write **both** if both historians would agree with the statement.

> **A**   **Historian A** would agree with the statement.
>
> **B**   **Historian B** would agree with the statement.
>
> **N**   **Neither** historian would agree with the statement.

_____1.   Businessmen should charge the same rates to all customers, regardless of how much or how regularly a customer buys (or ships).

_____2.   People should be judged according to the values and beliefs of the time period in which they live, not the values of later generations.

_____3.   It is wrong for businessmen to make secret deals. All deals should be open to the public.

4.   The government should take action to prevent businessmen from:

> _____a.   Making excess profits
>
> _____b.   Cheating the public
>
> _____c.   Forming monopolies
>
> _____d.   Hurting people's health

_____5.   A businessman who has an advantage over competitors is justified in using that advantage to run competitors out of business.

_____6.   A wildly competitive industry in which there are many companies, most of which are losing money, is worse than an industry in which there are only a few companies earning a stable profit.

Questions about Standard Oil/Rockefeller

 How do the two interpretations answer each of the following questions about Standard Oil and John D. Rockefeller? If a viewpoint does not answer the question, put an X after that historian. After you put down the historian's answer to a question, list the evidence, if any, that the historian uses to support his answer.

1.   What was the main reason for Rockefeller's success?
   a.   Historian A—

[Continued on next page.]

[Continued from previous page.]

Historian A's evidence—

b. Historian B—

Historian B's evidence—

2. Was Rockefeller wrong to accept rebates?
    a. Historian A—

    Historian A's evidence—

    b. Historian B—

    Historian B's evidence—

3. Standard Oil bought out or knocked out almost all of its oil refining competitors.
    Was it fair in its dealings with competitors?
    a. Historian A—

    Historian A's evidence—

    b. Historian B—

    Historian B's evidence—

LESSON 17 What Were Conditions Like for Workers in the Meat-packing Industry around 1900?

This lesson focuses on the historical question of what conditions were like for workers in the late-nineteenth and early-twentieth century. In answering this question you will have to evaluate sources carefully, especially when looking at historical novels as sources of information.

Historical Novels

People read novels for a number of reasons. One reason is for enjoyment. A second reason is to gain insights about some aspects of life. When you read novels in English class, you examine the literary elements of them, such as plot, character development, symbolism, and writing style. You may also look at the historical situation at the time the novel was written, and you might question why the author wrote it.

Historical novels, in addition to literary aspects, have an entirely different dimension as well. Historical novels deal with specific time periods, events, or people in history. As such, whether they mean to or not, historical novels influence our view of history. For example, our view of slavery, Southern culture, and the Civil War will probably be influenced by reading *Gone with the Wind*. After all, after reading the novel, some of the people we know best or identify with most from the South are Scarlett O'Hara, Rhett Butler, and the other characters. This same influence is present when historical novels are made into movies or docudramas.

When historians write interpretations which influence our view of history, we are on guard and subject their viewpoints to close scrutiny. We watch for assumptions and certain kinds of language, we evaluate their reasoning and evidence, and we compare their arguments to what we already know. It would be inconsistent not to subject historical novels to the same kind of scrutiny. What we are doing is evaluating the historical arguments in the novel, not judging the literary worth of the novel. Because historical novels are in a different form from regular historical arguments, our evaluation of them will take a different form from our analysis of historical arguments.

In the space below, list at least two questions that you could ask about a historical novel in order to judge the historical argument in it, and at least two places where you would look (be specific) to find more information on the novel.

Two questions

1.

2.

Two places to look

1.

2.

[Continued on next page.]

[Continued from previous page.]

Part I—How Accurate Is *The Jungle* in Describing the Meat-packing Industry?

In this part of the lesson you will be answering the question: How accurate is *The Jungle* in its description of life for Slavic immigrants in the Chicago meat-packing industry? Read each source and answer the questions that follow.

Source A

From: *Cliff's Notes, The Jungle,* by Frank H. Thompson, Jr. Lincoln, NE: Cliff's Notes, 1970. (*Cliff's Notes* are a critical commentary of the novel.)

I. *The Jungle* was published in 1906.

II. Upton Sinclair was given $500 by the socialist weekly magazine, *Appeal to Reason*, to investigate labor conditions in the Chicago stockyards and then publish his findings in the magazine. (Socialists are generally critical of conditions in capitalist countries such as the United States.)

III. Sinclair spent seven weeks living with workmen to gather information for the novel.

IV. After Sinclair had his findings printed in *Appeal to Reason* in article form, he went to a publisher to have it printed in novel form. The publisher refused to print it unless Sinclair made specific cuts in the manuscript.

V. Sinclair went to a second publisher, who checked on the truth of his observations, felt satisfied with them, and published the book.

VI. Reviews of the book in 1906:

A. *Arena*, June 1906: "This is one of the strongest and most powerful voices of protest against a great wrong that has appeared in America."

B. *Bookman*, April 1906: "It is impossible to withhold admiration of Mr. Sinclair's enthusiasm; and yet, many socialists will regret his mistaken advocacy of their cause. His reasoning is so false, his disregard for human nature so naive, his statement of facts so biased, his conclusions so perverted, that the effect can be only to disgust many honest, sensible folk with the very terms he uses so glibly."

C. *New York Times Saturday Review*, March 3, 1906: "We are afraid Mr. Sinclair has not been divinely appointed to be a deliverer of Labor lying prostrate. Somehow, in his tones the ear continuously catches the false note. He has been at pains to 'get up' his facts thoroughly, and his realism is often striking. But he seems to write not from the heart but from the head."

D. *Independent*, March 24, 1906: "Though overdrawn from a literary stand-point and almost surely exaggerated as to facts, [it] is a powerful and harrowing narrative. *The Jungle* may do some harm; also, it will surely do much good."

[Continued on next page.]

[Continued from previous page.]

1. Based on this information, was Upton Sinclair an accurate reporter in *The Jungle* of the situation in Chicago?

Source B

From: The Neill-Reynolds Commission Report of 1906. (The President ordered an investigation of the meat-packing industry which was led by Mr. Neill and Mr. Reynolds. This is their report to the President.)

The President:

As directed by you, we investigated the conditions in the principal establishments in Chicago engaged in the slaughter of cattle, sheep, and hogs and in the preparation of dressed meat and meat food products. Two and a half weeks were spent in the investigation in Chicago, and during this time we went through the principal packing houses in the stock-yards district, together with a few of the smaller ones. We have made no statement as a fact in the report here presented that was not verified by our personal examination. Certain matters which we were unable to verify while in Chicago are still under investigation. The following is therefore submitted as a partial report touching upon those practices and conditions which we found most common and not confined to a single house or class of houses. A more detailed report would contain many specific instances of defects found in particular houses.

CONDITION OF THE YARDS

Before entering the buildings we noted the condition of the yards themselves as shown in the pavement, pens, viaducts, and platforms. The pavement is mostly of brick, the bricks laid with deep grooves between them, which inevitably fill with manure and refuse. Such pavement cannot be properly cleaned and is slimy and malodorous when wet, yielding clouds of ill-smelling dust when dry. The pens are generally uncovered except those for sheep; these latter are paved and covered. The viaducts and platforms are of wood. Calves, sheep, and hogs that have died en route are thrown out upon the platforms where cars are unloaded. On a single platform on one occasion we counted 15 dead hogs; on the next, 10 dead hogs. The only excuse given for delay in removal was that so often heard—the expense.

BUILDINGS

Lighting—The buildings have been constructed with little regard to either light or ventilation. The workrooms, as a rule, are very poorly lighted. A few rooms at the top of the buildings are well lighted because they cannot escape the light, but most of the rooms are so dark as to make artificial light necessary at all times. Many inside rooms where food is prepared are without windows, deprived of sunlight and without direct communication with the outside air. They may be best described as vaults in which the air rarely changes.

Ventilation—Systematic ventilation of the workrooms is not found in any of the

[Continued on next page.]

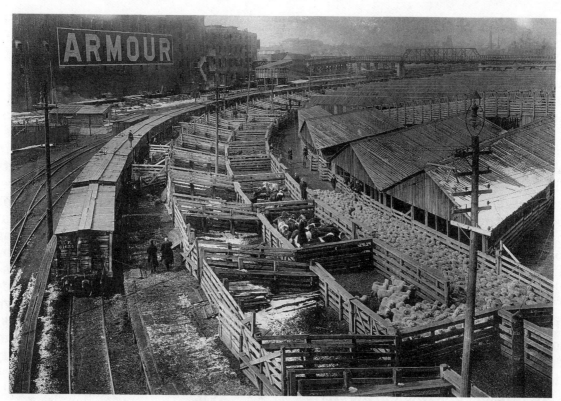

Chicago Stock Yards, 1907
Brown Brothers, Pennsylvania

Source B

[Continued from previous page.]

establishments we visited. In a few instances electric fans mitigate the stifling air, but usually the workers toil without relief in a humid atmosphere heavy with the odors of rotten wood, decayed meats, stinking offal, and entrails.

Equipment—The work tables upon which the meat is handled, the floor carts on which it is carried about, and the tubs and other receptacles into which it is thrown are generally of wood. In all the places visited but a single porcelain-lined receptacle was seen. Tables covered with sheet iron, iron carts, and iron tubs are being introduced into the better establishments, but no establishment visited has as yet abandoned the extensive use of wooden tables and wooden receptacles. These wooden receptacles are frequently found water

soaked, only half cleansed, and with meat scraps and grease accumulations adhering to their sides, and collecting dirt. This is largely true of meat racks and meat conveyors of every sort, which were in nearly all cases inadequately cleansed, and grease and meat scraps were found adhering to them, even after they had been washed and returned to service.

Sanitary conveniences—Nothing shows more strikingly the general indifference to matters of cleanliness and sanitation than do the privies (bathrooms) for both men and women. The prevailing type is made by cutting off a section of the workroom by a thin wooden partition rising to within a few feet of the ceiling. These privies usually ventilate

[Continued on next page.]

Source B

[Continued from previous page.]

into the workroom, a few are found with a window opening into the outer air. Many are located in the inside corners of the workrooms, and thus have no outside opening whatever. They are furnished with a row of seats, generally without even side partitions. These rooms are sometimes used as cloak-rooms by the employees. Lunch rooms constructed in the same manner, by boarding off a section of the workroom, often adjoin the privies, the odors of which add to the generally insanitary state of the atmosphere.

Abominable as the above-named conditions are, the one that affects most directly and seriously the cleanliness of the food products is the frequent absence of any lavatory provisions in the privies. Washing sinks are either not furnished at all or are small and dirty. Neither are towels, soap, or toilet paper provided. Men and women return directly from these places to plunge their unwashed hands into the meat to be converted into such food products as sausages, dried beef, and other compounds. Some of the privies are situated a long distance from the workrooms, and men relieve themselves on the killing floors or in a corner of the workrooms. Hence, in some cases the fumes of the urine swell the sum of nauseating odors arising from the dirty, blood-soaked, rotting wooden floors, fruitful culture beds for the disease germs of men and animals.

TREATMENT OF MEATS AND PREPARED FOOD PRODUCTS

Uncleanliness in handling products—An absence of cleanliness was also found everywhere in the handling of meat being prepared for the various meat products. After killing, carcasses are well washed, and up to the time they reach the cooling room are handled in a fairly sanitary and cleanly manner. The parts that leave the cooling room for treatment in bulk are also handled with regard to cleanliness, but the parts that are sent from the cooling room to those departments of the packing house in which various forms of meat products are prepared are handled with no regard whatever for cleanliness. In some of the largest establishments sides that are sent to what is known as the boning room are thrown in a heap upon the floor. The workers climb over these heaps of meat, select the pieces they wish, and frequently throw them down upon the dirty floor beside their working bench. Even in cutting the meat upon the bench, the work is usually pressed against their aprons, and these aprons were, as a rule, indescribably filthy. They were made in most cases of leather or of rough sacking and bore long accumulated grease and dirt. In only a few places were suitable oilcloth aprons worn. Moreover, men were seen to climb from the floor and stand, with shoes dirty from the refuse on the floors, on the tables upon which the meat was handled. They were seen at the lunch hour sitting on the tables on the spot on which the meat product was handled, and all this under the very eye of the superintendent of the room, showing that this was the common practice.

Meat scraps were also found being shoveled into receptacles from dirty floors where they were left to lie until again shoveled into barrels or into machines for chopping. These floors, it must be noted, were in most cases damp and soggy, in dark, ill-ventilated rooms, and the employees in utter ignorance of cleanliness or danger to health expectorated (spat) at will upon them. In a word, we saw meat shoveled from filthy wooden floors, piled on tables, rarely

[Continued on next page.]

Source B

[Continued from previous page.]

washed, pushed from room to room in rotten box carts, in all of which processes it was in the way of gathering dirt, splinters, floor filth, and the expectoration of tuberculous and other diseased workers. Where comment was made to floor superintendents about these matters, it was always the reply that this meat would afterwards be cooked, and that this sterilization would prevent any danger from its use. Even this, it may be pointed out in passing, is not wholly true. A very considerable portion of the meat so handled is sent out as smoked products and in the form of sausages, which are prepared to be eaten without being cooked.

TREATMENT OF EMPLOYEES

The lack of consideration for the health and comfort of the laborers in the Chicago stock yards seems to be a direct consequence of the system of administration that prevails. The various departments are under the direct control of superintendents who claim to use full authority in dealing with the employees and who seem to ignore all considerations except those of the account book. Under this system proper care of the products and of the health and comfort of the employees is impossible, and the consumer suffers in consequence. The insanitary conditions in which the laborers work and the feverish pace which they are forced to maintain inevitably affect their health. Physicians state that tuberculosis is disproportionately prevalent in the stock yards, and the victims of this disease expectorate on the spongy wooden floors of the dark workrooms, from which falling scraps of meat are later shoveled up to be converted into food products.

Much of the work in connection with the handling of meat has to be carried on in rooms of a low temperature, but even here a callous disregard was everywhere seen for the comfort of those who worked in these rooms. Girls and women were found in rooms registering a temperature of 38° F without any ventilation whatever, depending entirely upon artificial light. The floors were wet and soggy and in some cases covered with water, so that the girls had to stand in boxes of sawdust as a protection for their feet. In a few cases even drippings from the refrigerator rooms above trickled through the ceiling upon the heads of the workers and upon the food products being prepared. A very slight expense would have furnished drier floors and protected them against the tricklings from the ceiling. It was asserted by the superintendent of these rooms that this low temperature was essential to the proper keeping of the meat; but precisely similar work was found in other establishments carried on in rooms kept at a fair temperature. In many cases girls 16, 17, and 18 years old stand ten hours a day at work, much of which could be carried on while sitting down.

In several establishments well-managed restaurants were provided for the clerical force, and in one instance a smoking room was provided for them; but no provision was found anywhere for a place to eat for the male laborers. In pleasant weather they eat their luncheon sitting outdoors along the edge of the sidewalk, or any place where they can find standing room. In winter, however, and in inclement weather, their lunches have to be eaten in rooms that in many cases are stifling and nauseating. Eating rooms are provided in a number of places for women work-

[Continued on next page.]

Source B

[Continued from previous page.]

ers in the various departments; and in most of the large establishments coffee is served them at a penny a cup. Beyond this meager consideration for their convenience at meal times, scarcely any evidence is found that anyone gave a thought to their comfort.

James Bronson Reynolds
Charles P. Neill
Washington, D.C., June 2, 1906

2. On what points does the Neill-Reynolds Commission support the view of working conditions portrayed in *The Jungle*?

3. What points raised in *The Jungle* about working conditions does the Commission not support?

4. Which source is more reliable, *The Jungle* or the Commission Report? Why do you think so?

[Continued on next page.]

Stock Yards and Hyde Park Districts

Each square is a city block containing numerous buildings and many residents (people). Most street names have been omitted.

Union Stock Yards is where most of the meat-packing plants were located.

The heavy lines are railroads. Note that they surround the Stock Yards and run along Lake Michigan.

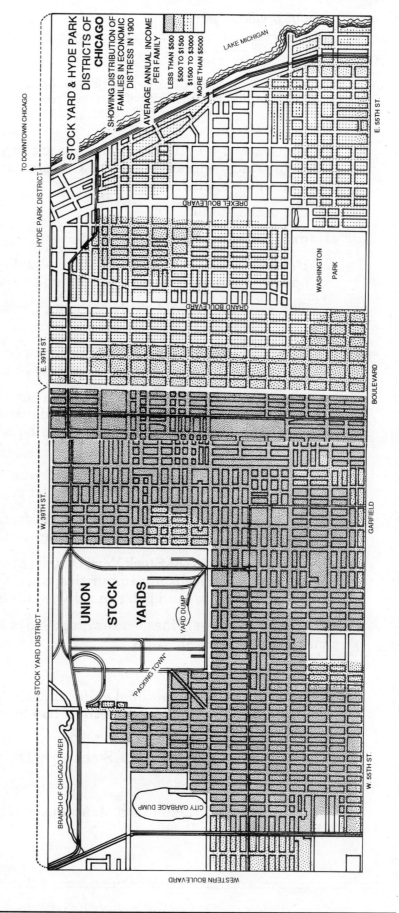

STOCK YARD & HYDE PARK
DISTRICTS OF **CHICAGO**

SHOWING DISTRIBUTION OF
FAMILIES IN ECONOMIC
DISTRESS IN 1900

AVERAGE ANNUAL INCOME
PER FAMILY

LESS THAN $500
$500 TO $1500
$1500 TO $3000
MORE THAN $5000

[Continued from previous page.]

Source C

From: *The Social Problem at the Chicago Stock Yards*, by Charles J. Bushnell.
(Ph.D. dissertation), Chicago: University of Chicago Press, 1902.

I. Author

    A. The author was a Ph.D. candidate in sociology at the University of Chicago, which is located near the Chicago Stock Yards. This dissertation was later published as a book.

    B. Beliefs of the author

        1. Freedom must be earned.

        2. Democracy means not just political equality but also equality of opportunity for every man to develop to his fullest capacity.

        3. The workman should study economics, restrict his drinking (alcoholic) habits, and educate his children.

        4. The owner should keep his temper, respect human nature, and pay just wages to his workers in a spirit of brotherhood.

II. Importance of Stock Yards—225,000 people earn their living directly from the one-mile-square Union Stock Yards, while another 225,000 make their living indirectly from the Stock Yards. The bulk of the population in the Stock Yard District is foreign.

III. A comparison of the Stock Yard District was made to Hyde Park, an adjoining, wealthier district. (See the map on page 117.)

IV. Mortality (death rate) is high in the Stock Yards, higher than in Hyde Park, as shown in Table 1 (next page). It is higher for the following reasons:

    A. Few of the streets in the Stock Yard District are paved. Some streets have wood paving which absorbs impurities, causing illness. Most streets are dirt which turns to mud holes in rainy weather.

    B. There are few sewer lines, so sewerage stays in the area. There is poor sanitation in general.

    C. The housing is run down.

    D. The food is poor in nutritional value, and the people choose poor foods. For example, many children at school had lunch boxes which contained only cakes and jellies.

    E. The city dump is located in the Stock Yard District. (See the map, p. 124)

V. Economic distress

    A. See the map for a comparison of income levels between the Stock Yard District and Hyde Park.

[Continued on next page.]

Source C

[Continued from previous page.]

B. Based on the Report of the Bureau of Associated Charities, there was a high rate in the Stock Yard District of families applying for charitable help in 1897 and 1900.

C. Drinking is a serious problem in the district, costing families a great deal of money. There are 500 saloons in the Stock Yard District compared to 21 in Hyde Park.

D. A diary of a manual laborer gives some information on the economic conditions of some families.

John Smith (fake name) and his wife were married in 1888 and had six children (born 1889, 1891, 1893, 1895, 1897, 1899). In the summer of 1898 Mr. Smith had no work for three months, and the family consequently came into sore need. Day after day he tramped the city from one end to the other, but without avail. Physically he is an able-bodied man, and is sober and faithful. But these facts were of no avail to him. In September 1898, he secured again his work in the yards, which place he kept for a year, with the

[Continued on next page.]

Table 1

Wards (Old Divisions)	Date	Total Number of Deaths	Deaths of Children under Five	General Death-rate per 1,000 of population	Proportion of Child Deaths to All Deaths	Number of Deaths by Six of the Chief Causes					
						Consumption	Pneumonia	Bronchitis	Typhoid Fever	Diptheria	Scarlet Fever
(Stock Yard) Twenty-Ninth Ward	1894	585	340	14.27	57%	51	60	44	14	23	9
	1895	582	248	14.81	42	38	71	27	16	29	4
	1896	612	308	15.57	58	60	59	31	14	40	3
	1897	515	243	13.10	47	65	59	24	6	17	2
	1898	576	252	14.37	43	71	72	33	8	7	2
	1899	649	262	14.83	40	73	100	20	9	27	28
	1900	644	261	15.62	40	68	116	27	10	16	11
(Hyde Park) Thirty-Second Ward	1894	437	129	9.10	29	53	37	8	9	12	4
	1895	540	133	9.08	24	48	51	12	12	26	5
	1896	551	125	10.18	22	48	46	18	18	10	0
	1897	601	133	11.11	22	47	50	14	21	19	2
	1898	656	124	11.89	18	48	66	19	19	14	1
	1899	719	141	11.84	19	60	76	18	14	13	18
	1900	774	146	11.18	19	60	95	20	10	8	22

SCHEDULE OF HEALTH STATISTICS OF TWENTY-NINTH, AND THIRTY-SECOND WARDS OF CHICAGO FOR YEARS 1894–1900
(From Reports of the Chicago Department of Health)

This table shows that in the 29th Ward of the Stock Yard District in 1894 there were 585 deaths. This was a rate of 14.27 per 1000 population (or 1.4% of the approximately 41,000 people in the 29th Ward in that year). Of the 585 deaths, 340 were children, about 57%. Of the 585 deaths, 51 were due to consumption, 60 were due to pneumonia, and so forth.

Source C

[Continued from previous page.]

exception of only two weeks in the following August. The work, however, was very irregular as regards time, varying from four or five hours a day to thirteen or fourteen. The wages received were twenty cents an hour. In September and the first of October 1899, work was slack; then for four weeks Mr. Smith worked overtime, until eight or nine o'clock in the evening, making twelve or thirteen dollars a week. He is always glad to work overtime, but the work tells severely on his nerves and hands. After November 1, work became slack again, then overtime once more about the middle of the month. Mr. Smith estimates that he averages about eight dollars a week for the entire year, or about $416 annual income; and this, he says, is better than a good many others do. In 1900 Mr. Smith was out of work six weeks in August and September. He expected to be out only two weeks, but at the end of that time the company kept his department closed two weeks longer, saying that they would start up again at the end of that time, but did not do so for two additional weeks. Mr. Smith said that he would have gotten permanent work elsewhere, but that if he did so he believed that he could never again work for the firm at the yards, however much he might need to. In the fall of 1900 he seemed to be much distressed over the short hours of work, only five or six hours per day, since his lack of employment in the summer had thrown the family into debt. In February 1901, Mrs. Smith fell ill, which necessitated doctor's bills. In March Mr. Smith was averaging seven dollars or less per week, and on March 11 the rooms where Mrs. Smith was still ill were cold. She was trying to economize in fuel, making a quarter of a ton of coal last two weeks instead of one. The domicile is in the four rear rooms of a first-story flat; the rent per month during the winter of 1900–1901 was $4; fuel per week cost $2.50; coal was bought by the quarter ton at $1.75; kerosene per week averaged 12 cents; groceries, $3; newspapers, 11 cents.

E. Working class wages are not increasing as fast as the wealth of other classes.

VI. Working conditions

A. Given the emphasis in business for making money and profits alone, it is safe to say companies would help themselves and hurt the workers. Unchecked by law or public pressure, companies would greatly lengthen working hours, reduce wages, limit air and light, and employ women and children, moving toward a barbarous stage of society. Some businessmen are recognizing the need for better conditions by introducing lunch rooms, toilet facilities, and ventilation for workers.

B. The sanitary conditions in the Chicago Stock Yards are much improved over former years, but there are still a lot of problems. The Chicago River (see maps pp. 117 and 124) is now better drained so more sanitary, but small animals can still make their way across the river on its coating of filth and grease. The dump is also still a menace to health.

[Continued on next page.]

Source C

[Continued from previous page.]

C. Workers need light, air, and cleanliness. A large proportion of the workmen at the yards are compelled to labor in cold, dark, damp passageways which scarcely ever see the glare of full sunlight.

D. In spite of the fact that the nature of the business makes necessary, especially in hot weather, an almost stifling volume of steam and overpowering odors in some departments, entirely inadequate provision is made, where the common workmen are employed, for ventilation, heating in winter, and cooling in summer.

E. The packing plants are clean in regards to the food packaged, but they are not clean in regards to the workers. Workers are not protected from machinery, steam, or odors and injurious fumes. For example, in the case of stuffing machines, the writer has seen a young girl thrusting her arm up to the elbow into a tube to arrange the meat, which a steam-driven piston rod plunging through the tube the next instant crowded into the can. Such careless methods of handling and running the machinery are not very uncommon, as has been repeatedly stated in the official reports of the Illinois state factory inspectors. There is one department of the packing house that is especially avoided by almost all the workmen, namely, the bone and fertilizer house, where in hot weather the odors and irritating dust are almost overpowering. In one week during November 1900, in one plant alone, 126 men were employed, and at the end of the week all but six had deserted—even in the face of extreme difficulty of securing work and maintaining a livelihood. The open vats and tanks in most of the large soap, oleo oil, butterine, and fertilizer houses are also places of annoyance and danger, where more than one man has lost his life by drowning or scalding.

F. Another element which hurts workers is the strain of the work. The strain is brought about by a process called "speeding up the gang." Most of the materials in process of production are attached upon trolleys or other machinery which keeps them in motion and requires each man to handle his part as it passes. By the employment of certain experienced and especially favored hands to set the pace, by the offer of shorter days of labor at approximately the same wages, and then later a reduction of the wages to correspond with the resulting reduction in time, the amount of work finally wrenched from the workmen is sometimes almost incredible, as well as inhuman. But this policy of virtually ignoring the interests of the workmen is more and more coming to appear as uneconomical to the most far-sighted employers.

Another matter directly relative to the health of the workmen is that of a place and opportunity for noon luncheon. The writer has gone through every department of all of the principal houses at the yards, and has visited them each many times, and nowhere has he found a single positively wholesome, cheerful, and adequate provision made for a place

[Continued on next page.]

Source C

[Continued from previous page.]

in which the common workmen could assemble to eat their lunches. Most of them stand about the corners of the buildings, or sit in the stairways to eat, if they do not go to the saloons which cluster so thickly about the yards. The saloons are massed at the entrances and exits of the Stock Yards. In the block just west of the yards, between Fortieth and Forty-first streets, there are thirteen saloons on one side of the street, where only one or two buildings devoted to another purpose are located. And there were counted in a single half-hour (during which the workmen of the yards are given time to eat their luncheon), being brought out of one of these saloons on the corner of Forty-first street and Ashland avenue, 1,065 pails of beer.

VII. To summarize, there are two important lessons to be learned from examination of the meat-packing industry in Chicago:

1. The present methods of private ownership and control of the means of production place the large body of wage-workers in such a position that practically none of them, however sober and thrifty they may individually be, can be the arbiters of their own happiness and destiny in the degree to which their employers can be the arbiters of theirs. Under our modern conditions of congested population and vast consolidation of business, the private ownership of the machine is practically the private ownership of the man who must use it if he is to keep from starving. This is the state of affairs which necessarily puts one class of citizens in a position of cringing subservience to another. It is therefore a condition intolerable to democracy.

2. Another difficulty of the situation, as old as humanity itself, and quite as much opposed to democracy as the first, is the prostitution of public office by the owners of large wealth. If class ownership of the tools is class ownership of the workmen, class control of the public offices is class control of the whole community.

5. To what extent does this dissertation on the Stock Yards support *The Jungle* on each of the following points? Explain your answers.

   a. Living conditions—

   b. Mortality (death) rate—

[Continued on next page.]

[Continued from previous page.]

   c. Poverty (economic distress)—

   d. Working conditions (sanitary conditions, light and air, work pace)—

   e. Economic and political power of the owners—

6.   What is the bias, or perspective, of the author of this dissertation? Considering the author's bias, how reliable is this source?

7.   Table 1 is used to make the point that the health of people in the Stock Yard District is worse than in Hyde Park and that changes should be made to improve conditions in the Stock Yard District.

   a. Evaluate the comparison.

   b. Evaluate the generalization about the number of deaths.

[Continued on next page.]

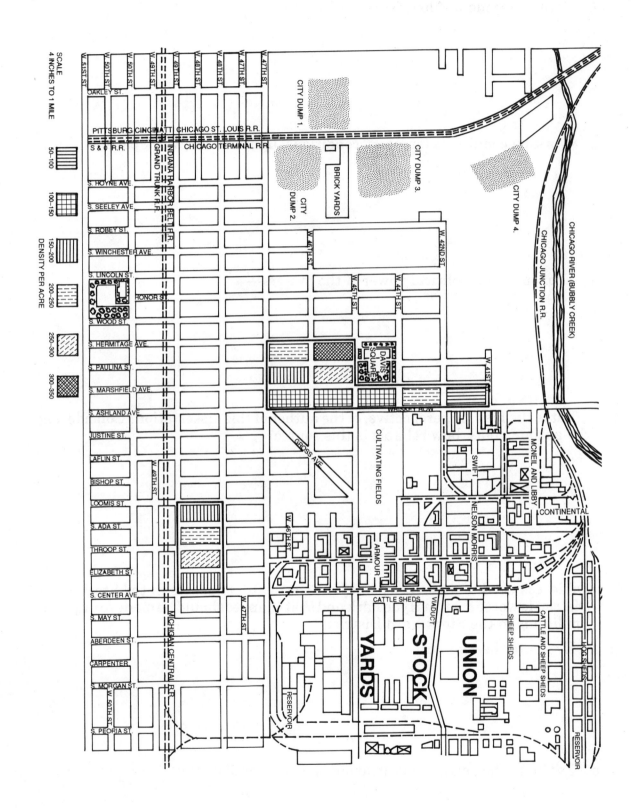

[Continued from previous page.]

Source D

From: Sophonisba P. Breckinridge and Edith Abbott, "Housing Conditions in Chicago, Ill.: Back of the Yards," *The American Journal of Sociology*, Volume XVI, No. 4, January 1911, pp. 433–68.

I. A study of housing conditions in the Stockyards District of Chicago reported in *Tenement Conditions in Chicago*, published by the City Homes Association (8 volumes):

"The Stockyards District and portions of South Chicago show outside insanitary conditions as bad as any in the world. Indescribable accumulations of filth and rubbish, together with the absence of sewerage, makes the surroundings of every dilapidated frame cottage abominably insanitary....

"Many working people have bought, or have tried to buy, these houses, but before they paid up the installments the houses were in very bad repair and wretchedly dilapidated. Very often workmen have tried to buy them on the installment plan and have lost them again and again....Very few of the houses in this locality are deficient in provision for light and ventilation, and none of them seem to be overcrowded. The worst features are the external conditions which surround the dwellings. In many parts of the district there are no sewers and the sewage from the houses stands in stagnant pools. The South branch of the Chicago River is really a ditch which accumulates a great deal of sewage from the Stockyards, and fills the air with poisonous odors. The stench from the Stockyards is always present. The district is overshadowed by heavy clouds of smoke from 'the Yards.'"

II. The Neill-Reynolds Commission Report of 1906 described the insanitary working conditions in the packing plants.

III. The Stockyards District is known to have a high rate of infant mortality, tuberculosis, poverty, bad housing, and poor sanitary conditions. One river is so polluted it is called "Bubbly Creek."

IV. This report is based on a door-to-door survey of the people living in the Stockyards District (see map p. 124) done by nine research students of the University of Chicago School of Civics and Philanthropy in 1909–10. The areas surveyed are in three neighborhoods (the shaded buildings on the map)—one is Polish, one Lithuanian, and one has a high number of lodgers. Some findings are:

A. There is a lot of open space (vacant lots) but the buildings are over-crowded, often due to lodgers living with families. There was an average of three lodgers per family. We found 1,981 cases of illegal overcrowding.

B. In some cases four people slept in a room that was actually too small for one person to sleep legally. In many apartments every room, including the kitchen, was used for sleeping. Many people slept in windowless rooms.

[Continued on next page.]

Source D

[Continued from previous page.]

C. In these three neighborhoods 2,393 out of 8,731 residents were lodgers. Many of the lodgers (adult male workers) slept in the same room as family members, some slept in the same bed.

D. About 1/4 of the families pay less than $7.00 per month rent; more than 1/2 the families pay less than $9.00 per month rent; $12.00 per month is about the highest rent in this area; 80% of the apartments had four or more rooms.

E. About 1/2 of the families claim to own their homes (3-floor tenement buildings) but most have a mortgage—they will lose the home eventually. Those who do own live in the basement (damp and unhealthy) or attic so they can rent out the best floors and make the most money.

F. Only 1/4 of the families had private toilets. Many used privy vaults and yard water closets which are illegal. We found several cases where more than 20 individuals were using a single water closet.

G. There are many saloons in the area.

H. The dumps (see the map) are huge open pits which hurt the health of residents. Women and children pick through the garbage at the dump.

8. To what extent does this study on housing conditions (including the quote in Roman Numeral I from the study by the Homes Association) support the view of living conditions portrayed in *The Jungle*? (Note points supported and not supported.)

9. Evaluate the source as a generalization about living conditions for Polish and Lithuanian workers in the Chicago Stock Yard District.

[Continued on next page.]

 ©1991 Midwest Publications/Critical Thinking Press & Software, P.O. Box 448, Pacific Grove, CA 93950

[Continued from previous page.]

Source E

From: *Wages and Family Budgets in the Chicago Stock-Yards District*, by J.C. Kennedy and Others. Chicago: University of Chicago Press, 1914.

I. The Stock-Yards District

A. The Chicago Stock Yards increased its business dramatically after 1865. By 1894 Chicago packaged more meat than the next three areas (Kansas City, East St. Louis, and Omaha) combined.

B. There were 75 people per acre in the Stock-Yards District, many of whom were Slovaks, Poles, and Lithuanians.

II. Wages and Earnings in the Packing Houses

A. Wages were figured by examining the payrolls of two of the largest packing companies, by looking at the reports of timekeepers, and by interviewing 350 employees in different departments at the companies.

[Continued on next page.]

Table 2

Rates of Wages Paid by Company 3	
Cents per hour	Percent
12	1.49
15	12.99
$16\frac{1}{2}$	29.39
$17\frac{1}{2}$	25.32
$18\frac{1}{2}$	2.79
20	9.35
$22\frac{1}{2}$	4.86
$23\frac{1}{2}$	.59
25	3.47
$26\frac{1}{2}$	1.24
$27\frac{1}{2}$	2.97
29	.42
30	2.11
$32\frac{1}{2}$	1.27
35	1.06
$37\frac{1}{2}$	.17
46	.13
50	.38
TOTAL	100.00%

Table 2 shows that 1.49% of the employees made 12¢ per hour, 12.99% made 15¢ per hour, etc.

[Continued from previous page.]

Table 3

Actual Earnings of 250 Employees in One of the Largest Packing Houses—1910		
Income per Year in Dollars	Number of Employees	Percentage of All Cases Tabulated
251–300	6	2.2%
301–350	4	1.6
351–400	8	3.2
401–450	10	4.0
451–500	14	5.6
501–550	32	12.8
551–600	53	21.2
601–650	17	6.8
651–700	21	8.4
701–750	23	9.2
751–800	15	6.0
801–850	14	5.8
851–900	13	5.2
901–950	15	6.0
951–1,000	5	2.0

The average yearly wage of these 250 employees was $634.80, or $12.20 per week.

Table 3 shows that 6 of the employees surveyed (2.2% of all employees surveyed) earned between $251–300 in 1910, 4 earned between $301–350, and so on.

[Continued on next page.]

Source E

[Continued from previous page.]

    B. Wages of workers in Chicago packing houses is shown in tables 2 and 3 (pp. 127–28).

    C. The wages of the mass of unskilled workers in the packing industry seem to have been reduced or at least have remained practically the same between 1903 and 1910, while the cost of living increased 16.5%.

    D. Of 170 husbands that we studied who were working, 53 lost an average of 10.9 weeks of work per year. Meat-packing workers in Chicago averaged 34 to 40 hours per week, combining some weeks over 40 hours during busy times with weeks below 30 hours at slack times.

    E. Family income of foreign workers in the Chicago Packing Houses is given below (Table 4). These are almost all unskilled workers. Every family did not have children working (only 50 out of 184 families had children working) or lodgers so the amounts for these columns are not what the families actually made but the average of all the families (including those who did not have working children or lodgers).

    F. Family of five incomes and expenditures (expenses) were as follows:

Altogether there were 34 families of five members, having an average income of $801.49, with an average expenditure of $748.88. Eight of the families had deficits averaging $47.25. In practically every case where the family income went below $600 there was a deficit. This does not mean, however, that a family of five can live on $600 a year. They may exist on that amount for a time, but they cannot live on it. The least misfortune will plunge them into debt and sooner or later they will become dependent on charity. (See Table 5, p. 130.)

[Continued on next page.]

Table 4

		Sources of Income per Family				
	Husband	Children 14–15 Years Old	Other Members of Family	Lodgers	Other Sources	Totals (Per Family)
Polish	$447.46	$67.48	$279.50	$41.56	$33.39	$869.39
Lithuanian	503.55	35.38	48.91	180.46	36.30	804.60
Miscellaneous	425.63	59.38	382.84	33.84	24.77	926.46
All families	464.87	54.38	210.01	91.72	33.15	854.13

Table 4 shows that, on average, Polish adult male workers earned about $447, but $422 earned by children, other family members, and other sources brought the average family income to $869.

[Continued from previous page.]

Table 5

Annual Expenses*

Rent	$120.00	$12 per month for 4 sanitary rooms
Heat and light	36.00	an average of $3.00 per month
Bread and baked goods	72.00	20 cents per day
Butter	20.28	$1\frac{1}{2}$ lbs. per week at 26 cents per pound
Lard	3.90	$\frac{1}{2}$ pound per week at 15 cents per pound
Cheese	10.40	1 lb. per week at 20 cents per pound
Eggs	19.50	$1\frac{1}{2}$ dozen per week at 25 cents per dozen
Milk	43.80	$1\frac{1}{2}$ quarts per day at 8 cents per quart
Sugar	9.18	3 lbs. per week at 6 cents per pound
Meat	87.60	$1\frac{1}{2}$ lbs. per day at 16 cents per pound
Fish	11.96	$1\frac{1}{2}$ lbs. per week at 15 cents per pound
Vegetables	36.50	10 cents per day
Fruits	26.00	50 cents per week
Cereals	7.80	15 cents per week
Pickles, pepper, spices, etc.	5.20	10 cents per week
Coffee, tea, etc.	13.00	25 cents per week
	$523.12	total for rent, heat, and foodstuffs
Clothing, father	30.00	1 suit clothes, working-clothes, shirts, underwear, shoes, and sundries
Clothing, mother	30.00	includes dresses, coats, winter garments, shoes, hats, etc.
Clothing, children	40.00	includes dresses, coats, winter garments, shoes, hats, etc.
Carfare	10.40	20 cents per week
Education	15.00	includes children's books and newspapers
Laundry	5.20	10 cents per week
Soap, starch, etc.	13.00	25 cents per week
Furniture and furnishings	22.00	includes household utensils, brooms, etc.
Insurance	24.50	husband, 15 cents weekly, wife and 3 children, each 5 cents per week
Health	10.00	includes all doctors' bills and medicines
Societies and trade unions	10.40	20 cents per week
	$210.50	total for miscellaneous
+	523.12	total for rent, heat, etc. (from above)
Total Expenditures	$733.62	

*Note: The values in this table are quoted directly from the source. The source offers no explanation for mathematical inconsistencies.

[Continued on next page.]

©1991 Midwest Publications/Critical Thinking Press & Software, P.O. Box 448, Pacific Grove, CA 93950

Source E

[Continued from previous page.]

III. Earnings of Unskilled Workers in Industries Outside of the Chicago Stock Yards

    A. Earnings of unskilled workers in Chicago tailor shops are shown in Table 6 (p. 132).

    B. Earnings of unskilled workers in Kansas City meat-packing houses are shown in Table 7 (p. 132).

    C. Earnings of unskilled male workers in the iron and steel industry are shown in Table 8 (p. 133).

IV. Summary of Significant Facts

One hundred and eighty-four families were studied: 88 Polish, 68 Lithuanian, 28 miscellaneous.

Average size of family, 5.33. In addition, on an average, 1.09 lodgers per family.

In 94 families the father was the only wage-earner; in 52 families children fourteen to fifteen were at work; in 21 families the wife was at work; 92 families obtained an income from lodgers.

The income of 110 families was $800 per year or less; the income of 74 families was over $800 per year; the average income of all families was $854.13.

The average wage of all husbands was $503.15. Fifty-three husbands lost 580 solid weeks of work or, on an average, 10.9 weeks per year.

In the 52 families where children were at work the average income derived from this source was $200.14 per year.

One hundred and thirty-one families rented their quarters. The average rental per family was $107.83, or 13.2 percent of the total expenditure. One hundred of the 131 renting families occupied flats of four rooms.

The 68 Lithuanian families had on an average 4.12 lodgers per family. In one case 13 people were crowded together in four small basement rooms.

The average expenditure for foodstuffs and liquors was $441.83 per family, or 53.62 percent of the total expenditure.

One hundred and eighty families used alcoholic liquors; the average annual expenditure per family was $36.42, or 4.42 percent of the total expenditure.

The minimum amount necessary to support a family of five efficiently in the Stock Yard District is $800 per year, or $15.40 per week.

[Continued on next page.]

[Continued from previous page.]

Table 6

Percentage of Employees In Tailor Shops Sixteen Years of Age and Over Earning Less Than Specified Amounts In a Representative Week, by Sex (Chicago)						
	Percentage of Employees Earning Under					
	$2.00	$4.00	$6.00	$8.00	$10.00	$12.00
Males	3.0	9.1	20.7	36.5	49.5	61.7
Females	2.8	13.4	37.5	61.2	80.2	90.6

Table 7

Numbers of Men, Women, and Children Earning Classified Amounts, and Percentages of the Total Number Earning Specified Amounts in Slaughtering and Packing Establishments (Kansas City, 1909) (19 Establishments)*						
Earnings per Week	Wage Earners	Men (Sixteen and over)		Women (Sixteen and over)	Children	Percentage of Total Wage Earners
		Number of men	Percentage of men			
Under $5	222	134	1.23%	46	42	1.86%
$5–8.99	1,681	1,043	9.55	493	171	14.13
9–9.99	2,884	2,820	25.84	38	...	24.23
10–11.99	3,113	2,972	27.23	141	...	26.16
12–14.99	2,265	2,227	20.41	38	...	19.03
15–19.99	1,333	1,316	12.06	17	...	11.23
$20 and over	401	401	3.68	...	...	3.36
TOTALS	11,899	10,913	100.00%	773	213	100.00%

*Kansas Bureau of Labor and Industry, Annual Report, 1909, p. 26.

Table 7 shows weekly wage earnings of meat-packing workers in 19 packing companies in Kansas City—222 workers (134 men, 46 women, and 42 children) earned less than $5 per week. This was 1.86% of all the workers surveyed (11,899) and so on.

[Continued on next page.]

[Continued from previous page.]

Table 8

Average Amount of Weekly Earnings of Male Employees Eighteen Years of Age and over of Certain Slavic and South-European Races in the Iron and Steel Industry (Foreign Born)				
Race	Average Weekly Earnings		Race	Average Weekly Earnings
Croatian	$11.02		Serbian	$10.75
Dalmatian	11.44		Slovak	12.27
Lithuanian	12.89		Slovenian	11.85
Rumanian	11.06		Polish	12.69
Russian	12.05			

This condensed table suggests that the average weekly wages of the unskilled workers in iron and steel are in the neighborhood of $12—a higher average certainly than corresponding employees in the Chicago packing houses would show. But employees in the Chicago packing houses do not regularly work 72 or 84 hours a week, nor is there any such steadiness of employment in the packing houses as is the case in the steel mills.

10. To what extent does this book on wages and budgets support *The Jungle* on each of the following points? Explain your answers.

   a. Wages of Lithuanian workers, and number of hours worked—

   b. The possibility of Lithuanian workers meeting family expenses—

[Continued on next page.]

[Continued from previous page.]

    c. Children working—

    d. Overcrowding—

    e. Alcohol abuse—

11. How did the wages of unskilled workers in the Chicago Stock Yards (Tables 3 and 4) compare to those of unskilled workers in the following:

    a. Tailor shops in Chicago (Table 6)—

    b. Meat packing in Kansas City (Table 7)—

    c. The steel industry (Table 8)—

[Continued on next page.]

[Continued from previous page.]

12. Are the wages of unskilled workers in the Chicago Stock Yards representative of the wages of unskilled workers throughout the United States around 1900?

13. How reliable is this source?

Part II—How Accurately Does *The Jungle* Describe Conditions for All Workers?

Did the novel *The Jungle* influence your opinion about the plight of Lithuanian immigrants in the meat-packing industry around 1900, the plight of Lithuanian immigrants in general, the plight of immigrants in general, the meat-packing industry, industrialization in the nineteenth century in general, or other topics? These are very different topics. That is, *The Jungle* may be accurate in its portrayal of Lithuanian immigrants in the meat-packing industry around 1900, but inaccurate in its portrayal of other immigrant groups or of workers in other industries. If your opinion about industrialization in general was influenced, you have to ask yourself how representative the descriptions in this novel were of industrialization in the United States in general.

This idea of representativeness has to do with generalizing (pp. 8–10 in the "Guide to Critical Thinking"). The graph on the next page describes the novel as a sample of different levels of generalization having to do with conditions of workers in various industries.

Keep in mind that Jurgis was an unskilled worker and many workers were skilled. This further complicates any generalizations.

If you decided that the descriptions in *The Jungle* were basically accurate, you might conclude that "Lithuanian immigrants in the meat-packing industry around 1900 had terrible working conditions." If you concluded that "workers in the United States around 1900 had terrible working conditions," however, you are on much shakier ground. This generalization applies to the largest circle (see graph, next page), yet it is derived from the sample of the smallest circle. How do we know, for example, that non-immigrant textile workers in Lawrence, Massachusetts had anything like the same conditions as described in *The Jungle*? Everything in *The Jungle* could be true, but the second generalization above ("workers in the United States") could be false. The warning is: "Don't overgeneralize from one case or a small sample."

Look at the information from Source F (next page) about Slavic immigrants in the steel mills and answer the questions that follow.

[Continued on next page.]

[Continued from previous page.]

Graph 1　Workers in the United States about 1900*

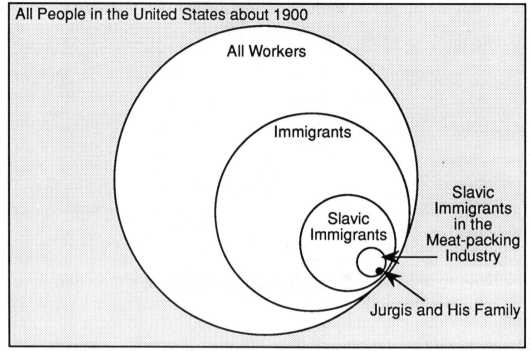

All People in the United States about 1900

All Workers

Immigrants

Slavic Immigrants

Slavic Immigrants in the Meat-packing Industry

Jurgis and His Family

* Not to scale.

Source F

From: "Slavic Immigrants in the Steel Mills" by David Brody (Historian) in *The Private Side of American History*, 1975, pp. 127–39.

I. During 1900–1915 there were 9.5 million immigrants from Southern and Eastern Europe (Slavic peoples).

II. Wages in the Steel industry

   A. $1.50–2.00 per day, which was not enough to support a wife and children.

   B. A family requires $15 per week to live. Two-thirds of recent immigrants made less than $12.50 per week, one-third made less than $10.00 per week.

   C. The Pittsburgh Association of Charities found in 1910 that if a steel worker worked 12 hours per day every day of the year, he could not provide a family of five with the barest necessities.

   D. Many families had boarders (lodgers) to supplement their incomes.

III. However:

   A. Most immigrants were single men who came expecting to go back to Europe in a few years with a lot of money.

[Continued on next page.]

Source F

[Continued from previous page.]

    B. The Immigration Commission reported that one-third of the immigrants were single, and three-fourths of the married men who had been here less than five years had wives abroad. (That is, they were here alone.)

    C. Immigrants in the steel industry sent home thousands of dollars.

    D. There were 30,000 immigrants working in the steel industry.

IV. Conditions

    A. An immigrant stated: "Here in America, one must work for three horses."

    B. Hungarian churchman inspecting Pittsburgh steel mills: "Wherever the heat is most insupportable, the flames most scorching, the smoke and soot most choking, there we are certain to find compatriots [other Hungarians] bent and wasted with toil."

    C. Immigrant: "There are different kinds of work, heavy and light, but a man from our country cannot get the light."

    D. In general, only the hardier men from Europe came to America.

    E. An immigrant stated: "The work is heavy but I don't mind it. Let it be heavy, but may it last without interruption." (Brick factory worker)

    F. Russian steel laborers in Pittsburgh told an investigator they were glad to work extra days.

    G. The Pittsburgh Survey, 1909–14, stated that a majority of Slavic workers voluntarily reported on Sundays in 1907 to clear yards and repair equipment.

    H. The accident rate for non-English speaking workers at the South Works 1906–10 was twice the average of all workers.

    I. Almost one-fourth of recent immigrants in the steel works each year— 3,273 in five years—were injured or killed.

    J. In one year 127 Eastern Europeans died in steel mills. (Pittsburgh Survey, Volume II—Work Accidents)

    K. Accidents wiped out savings. Pennsylvania courts ruled that liability statutes did not apply to non-resident aliens. (That is, owners did not have to pay for injuries to immigrants.)

V. Living Conditions

    A. Immigrants lived on poor, swampy land called "Hunkeyvilles." Steel companies collected 200% of their investment in shanties (shacks) per year in rents. Most people made 5%–10% profit per year on bonds and investments through banks. At 200%, an investment of $1000 would be $3000 in one year!

[Continued on next page.]

Source F

[Continued from previous page.]

    B. The Pittsburgh Board of Health Report, 1907, described flimsy, beaten shacks with crude sanitary conditions for Slavic immigrants.

    C. Housing was greatly overcrowded. For example, there were 33 Serbians in five rooms.

    D. Ignorance made it worse. Immigrants did not boil water, drank from rivers, and got typhoid.

    E. Immigrants paid an average of 20% more per room than English-speaking tenants. Landlords made no repairs.

    F. Alderman courts cheated immigrants. On pay day they would haul immigrants into courts on dubious charges (like jaywalking) and make them pay fines.

VI. Immigration and Emigration Trends and Social Mobility of Immigrants

    A. When work was good, more immigrants came. When work was bad, many left.

    B. During 1908–10, 44 Southern and Eastern Europeans left for every 100 that arrived.

    C. Many workers stayed in the United States because there were no classes as in Europe and because they achieved upward mobility.

Table 9

Number of years the worker has been in the United States	Skilled	Semiskilled	Unskilled	% of workers making over $15.00 per week
Under 2 years	0	56	314	under 10%
2–5 years	17	243	544	under 10%
5–10 years	79	441	475	13–25%
over 10 years	184	398	439	20–33%

Table 9 is based on a survey of workers in 1910. Workers were asked how long they had lived in the United States—370 said they had lived here under 2 years. Of those, none were skilled workers, 56 were semiskilled, 314 were unskilled, and less than 10% made more than $15.00 per week. Of those who said they were in the United States 2–5 years, 17 were skilled, and so on.

From: *Labor Conditions*—U.S. Bureau of Labor, *Report on Conditions of Employment in the Iron and Steel Industry.* Appendix C, p. 480ff.

[Continued on next page.]

[Continued from previous page.]

14. Remembering that Jurgis (the main character in *The Jungle*) was married, had just moved to the United States, and was living with his family, how accurate is *The Jungle* in describing conditions for the following?

    a. Slavic immigrants in the steel industry—

    b. Workers in the steel industry—

15. To what extent does this source support *The Jungle* on each of the following?

    a. How dangerous the work was—

    b. Companies defrauding (ripping off) immigrants (for example, Jurgis buying the house)—

    c. Housing conditions—

    d. Government corruption and fraud—

[Continued on next page.]

[Continued from previous page.]

16. How reliable is Source F?

17. Novels, movies, and television dramas sometimes influence our views of historical topics. Why is it a good idea to be cautious about drawing conclusions from these sources?

[Continued on next page.]

How Accurate is *The Jungle*

As you read *The Jungle,* fill in the first column on the author's portrayal of conditions in the Chicago Stock Yard District as shown by the events that happen to Jurgis and his relatives. After you have filled in the first column, read sources A through E and fill in the second column.

Condition	How these conditions are portrayed in *The Jungle*	What sources A through E show about these conditions (After each note write the letter of the source.)
Working conditions (sanitation, light, air, chance of being injured, speed of work)		
Living conditions (sanitation, overcrowding, streets, light, heat, health care)		
Economic conditions (wages, ability for a family to survive and prosper)		
What owners were like (power of owners, did they cheat workers?)		
Political conditions (elections, corruption, police)		

LESSON 18   What Brought about the Progressive Movement?

The Progressive Movement was an era of reform from roughly 1900 to 1914 (the outbreak of World War I). The movement was comprised of a number of groups, many of whom lived in cities. The Progressives passed reforms to clean up government and regulate (rules that prevent businesses from doing certain things or forcing them to do things) businesses, mostly at the local and state levels but also at the national level. These reformers believed that the government had to take an active role to protect the common good. The Progressives created such reforms as the initiative, referendum, and recall to give more power to the people in government, and the Pure Food and Drug Law and Federal Trade Commission to regulate business. The three Progressive presidents were Theodore Roosevelt, William Howard Taft, and Woodrow Wilson.

In this lesson you will read three interpretations of what the driving force in the Progressive Movement was. Read the interpretations and answer the questions that follow.

Interpretation A

(1)   One of the main forces driving the Progressive Movement was the discovery, around 1900, that big business interests were corrupting politics in their efforts to gain special privileges. The outraged public acted to reform the situation. The Progressives moved to clean up the government and then to use government to clean up (through regulation) business.

(2)   There is abundant evidence showing this trend. The autobiographies of the leading Progressives, such as Theodore Roosevelt, Robert La Follette, and Lincoln Steffens, detail how their authors awakened to the corrupt alliance of business and government.[1] Muckraking magazines, which exposed the corruption, increased their circulation tremendously during this time. The newspaper editorials condemning big business privilege also show the public's concern with the issue.

(3)   The result of this focus of the public's attention was progressive legislation (laws) to reform big business practices.

Endnotes for Interpretation A

[1] Theodore Roosevelt, *An Autobiography* (New York, 1913), 85–86; Robert La Follette, *La Follette's Autobiography: A Personal Narrative of Political Experiences* (Madison, Wisconsin, 1960), 3–97; Lincoln Steffens, *The Autobiography of Lincoln Steffens* (New York, 1931), 357–627.

Interpretation B

(1)   For years historians have stated that an important part of the Progressive Movement was the outraged public's drive to stop big business's corruption of government. This view has misled us about the causes, intentions, and results of the progressive reforms. Actually, the Progressive Movement did much to encourage big business.

[Continued on next page.]

Interpretation B

[Continued from previous page.]

(2) While some people in the Progressive Movement were upset by business corruption in politics and wanted reform, this was not an all-important goal. First, corruption in government was certainly nothing new. Americans had always realized it existed. Second, the Progressive Movement was made up of more than just the poor people who were fed up with rich business privileges. There were several diverse groups in the movement, including businessmen and professionals, who wanted to help business, not control it.

(3) When one looks at the results of the progressive reforms against business, the picture becomes even clearer. What the Progressives set up were regulatory agencies to watch over business. These agencies were set up just like corporations, with groups of people working together (called bureaucracies). So, the Progressives actually accelerated the trend toward bigness by making government more like big business.

(4) Moreover, the regulatory agencies set up by the Progressives were controlled by business for the benefit of business. The progressive reforms looked like an attack on business when, in fact, the new laws actually were passed by businessmen to help business operate more efficiently.

Interpretation C

(1) At first, historians believed that the Progressive Movement passed business reforms in order to control business because the people were outraged by corruption in business and government. Then, a different group of historians argued that the progressive reforms were passed by businessmen in order to help business. These historians said the reforms actually speeded up the trend toward the corporate form which has dominated our society in the twentieth century. To these historians, the reforms were passed to satisfy the people so they would leave business alone.

(2) Most historians accept the second interpretation. The evidence shows, however, that the average people really were upset by reports of corruption and the reforms really were to control business.

(3) Americans had always believed that the government should give no special privileges to any individuals or groups. People knew that government could be a breeding ground for corruption. While there had been reports of scandals and corruption in government in the nineteenth century, the abuses disclosed in the first decade of the twentieth century were of an entirely different magnitude. Muckraking articles (articles that reveal corruption or scandals in government or business) revealed corruption in almost every area of government and business. Americans realized that the sheer size of big business was causing more serious problems. Industrialism, it seemed, had made business larger and stronger than government, making it easy for business to use government for its own special privileges. Progressives believed that reforms had to be passed to help the government control business rather than the other way around.[1]

(4) The evidence strongly indicates that it was the public's perception of big-business corruption which led to the reforms. The great bulk of muck-

[Continued on next page.]

Interpretation C

[Continued from previous page.]

raking articles on corruption were published in 1905 and 1906. Scandal after scandal was revealed in national magazines, local newspapers, and legislative halls across the country. The result was that party platforms and political leaders emphasized the issue in the years that followed.

(5) Everyone, it seemed, was now concerned with business corrupting government.[2] Table 1 below shows the dramatic increase in legislation to regulate business by state governments in the period after the muckraking articles.

(6) The main result of these reforms was to actually help business. Once government agencies were set up, the public lost interest in the reforms. In the meantime, businessmen gained control of the positions on the regulatory agencies, which is natural, since the businesses had the most interest in the regulations. The bureaucratic agencies accelerated the trend toward the corporate form, which also helped business in the long run. This does not mean, however, that the reforms were a fake passed by businessmen to help themselves and pacify the public. The evidence shows that the progressive business reforms were passed by a public outraged by the perceived corruption of government by big business. The fact that the reforms actually helped business should not lead us to the conclusion that the reforms were not originally passed to control business.

Table 1

[Continued on next page.]

Selected Categories of State Legislation 1903–08				
Type of Legislation	1903–04	1905–06	1907–08	Total 1903–08
Regulation of Lobbying	0	2	10	12
Prohibition of Corporate Campaign Contributions	0	3	19	22
Regulation or Prohibition of Free Railroad Passes for Public Officials	4	6	14	24
Mandatory Direct Primary	4	9	18	31
Regulation of Railroad Corporation by Commission	5	8	28	41
Totals	13	28	89	130

NOTE: Figures represent the number of states that passed legislation in the given category during the specified years.

From: New York Library, *Index of Legislation* (Albany, N.Y., 1904–9).

[Continued from previous page.]

Endnotes for Interpretation C

[1] Dewey W. Grantham, Jr., "The Progressive Era and the Reform Tradition," *Mid-America*, 46 (1964), 224–35.

[2] Examples: Republican platform, 1906: The Party was opposed to the "domination of corporate influences in public affairs." Democratic platform, 1906: "We favor the complete elimination of railway and other public service corporations from the politics of the state."

Q Interpretation A

1. What is the main point of Interpretation A?

2. One type of reasoning used in the argument is proof. List below the other two types of reasoning, the key questions (see the boxes on pages 5–10 in the "Guide to Critical Thinking"), and how well the argument answers these questions.

   A.

Type of Reasoning	Key Question	How Well Answered

   B.

Type of Reasoning	Key Question	How Well Answered

3. Write a description or draw a diagram of how this author views the Progressive Movement (for example, what groups made it up and how decisions were made).

[Continued on next page.]

[Continued from previous page.]

What is your judgment of this view of the makeup of the Progressive Movement?

4. Describe or draw a model of this author's view of the operation of politics.

What is your judgment of this view of how politics works?

5. How strong is the evidence given in endnote 1?

 Interpretation B

6. What is the main point of Interpretation B?

[Continued on next page.]

[Continued from previous page.]

7. List below the three types of reasoning used in this argument (refer to the paragraph indicated), the key questions, and how well the argument answers these questions.

    A. Paragraph 1

Type of Reasoning	Key Question	How Well Answered

    B. Paragraph 2, sentences 4 and 5

Type of Reasoning	Key Question	How Well Answered

    C. Paragraph 3

Type of Reasoning	Key Question	How Well Answered

8. Write a description or draw a diagram of how this author views the Progressive Movement.

[Continued on next page.]

[Continued from previous page.]

9. Write your opinion of why progressive reforms in the area of business were probably passed and how they affected business.

Q Interpretation C

10. What is the main point of Interpretation C?

11. List below the four kinds of reasoning used in this argument (refer to paragraphs and sentences indicated), the key questions, and how well the argument answers these questions.

   A. Paragraphs 1 and 2

Type of Reasoning	Key Question	How Well Answered

   B. Paragraph 3, sentence 3

Type of Reasoning	Key Question	How Well Answered

[Continued on next page.]

[Continued from previous page.]

C. Paragraph 4

Type of Reasoning	Key Question	How Well Answered

D. Paragraph 5, including Table 1

Type of Reasoning	Key Question	How Well Answered

12. Describe or draw a diagram of how this author views the Progressive Movement.

13. Describe or draw a diagram of the author's view of the operation of politics.

14. Write your opinion of why progressive reforms in the area of business were probably passed and how they affected business.

Unit 4
Workers, Immigrants, and Farmers in the Late 1800s

LESSON 19   Assessing the Strengths and Weaknesses of
                 Evidence

List the strengths and weaknesses of each piece of evidence, then circle the most
important strength or weakness. Refer to p. 3 for help in evaluating evidence.

Q Questions 1–3 deal with the question "Is the student telling the truth?"

1. Leana tells the teacher she lost the homework when it blew away on the way
    to school.

    STRENGTHS   WEAKNESSES

2. Philip tells the teacher he could not do his homework because he and his parents
    had to go to a wedding.

    STRENGTHS   WEAKNESSES

3. The teacher hears Lance tell another student that he watched the baseball
    game last night instead of doing his homework.

    STRENGTHS   WEAKNESSES

[Continued on next page.]

[Continued from previous page.]

 Questions 4–6 deal with the question "What were working conditions like in Lowell in the 1840s?"

4. A mill girl wrote in her diary for October 12, 1843, that the working conditions in Lowell were very good.

    STRENGTHS   WEAKNESSES

5. A mill owner in a letter to his wife said that due to competition he could not pay to improve the terrible working conditions at his mill.

    STRENGTHS   WEAKNESSES

6. A mill girl said in *The Lowell Offering* (a magazine run by the mill owners) that the working conditions were very good.

    STRENGTHS   WEAKNESSES

[Continued on next page.]

[Continued from previous page.]

 Questions 7–10 deal with the question "Who started the violence at the Homestead Steel Plant, the workers, or management?"

7. Henry Frick (manager of the Homestead Plant) said in a newspaper interview that the workers caused the violence.

STRENGTHS   WEAKNESSES

8. The *Encyclopedia Americana* says that management started the violence.

STRENGTHS   WEAKNESSES

9. A bystander told a reporter she saw the workers start the violence at the Homestead Plant. The bystander was a nurse.

STRENGTHS   WEAKNESSES

10. The union-run *Homestead Daily* said that Henry Frick started the violence.

STRENGTHS   WEAKNESSES

LESSON 20 Recognizing and Assessing Cause-and-Effect Reasoning

Part A

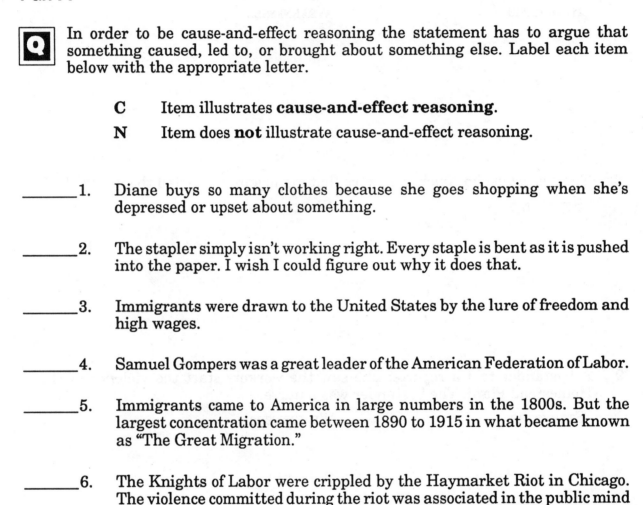

In order to be cause-and-effect reasoning the statement has to argue that something caused, led to, or brought about something else. Label each item below with the appropriate letter.

C Item illustrates **cause-and-effect reasoning**.

N Item does **not** illustrate cause-and-effect reasoning.

_____1. Diane buys so many clothes because she goes shopping when she's depressed or upset about something.

_____2. The stapler simply isn't working right. Every staple is bent as it is pushed into the paper. I wish I could figure out why it does that.

_____3. Immigrants were drawn to the United States by the lure of freedom and high wages.

_____4. Samuel Gompers was a great leader of the American Federation of Labor.

_____5. Immigrants came to America in large numbers in the 1800s. But the largest concentration came between 1890 to 1915 in what became known as "The Great Migration."

_____6. The Knights of Labor were crippled by the Haymarket Riot in Chicago. The violence committed during the riot was associated in the public mind with the Knights. As a result, public opinion went against the Knights.

Part B

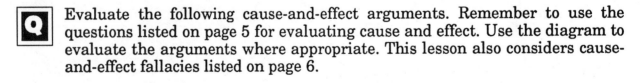

Evaluate the following cause-and-effect arguments. Remember to use the questions listed on page 5 for evaluating cause and effect. Use the diagram to evaluate the arguments where appropriate. This lesson also considers cause-and-effect fallacies listed on page 6.

7. "Last year, when we had one vice principal (a vice principal deals with discipline

[Continued on next page.]

[Continued from previous page.]

in a school) there were only two students suspended. Now with two vice principals we've had eight students suspended. That second guy caused the discipline in the school to fall apart."

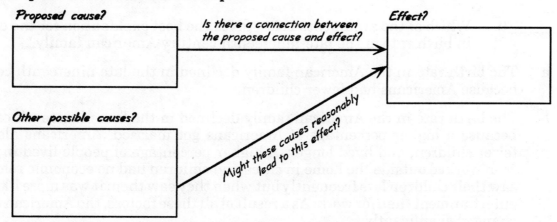

How strong is the reasoning in question 7? Why do you think so?

8. "Wherever you see slum areas in Homestead, or in the Ohio Valley in general, there you will see immigrants concentrated. Those foreigners are ruining the neighborhoods of the mill towns."

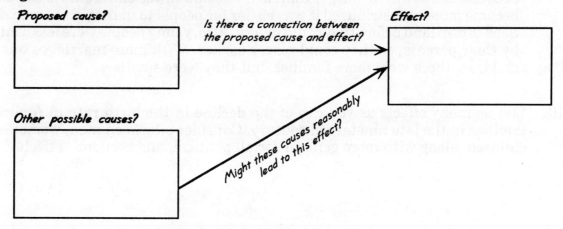

How strong is this reasoning? Why do you think so?

[Continued on next page.]

[Continued from previous page.]

 Declining Family Size

_____9.   Which of the arguments below gives the best explanation for the decline in birth rate in the late-nineteenth-century American family?

a.   The birth rate in the American family declined in the late nineteenth century because Americans had fewer children.

b.   The birth rate in the American family declined in the late nineteenth century because a higher percentage of Americans got married. Americans also had fewer children, and lived longer. A higher percentage of people lived in cities. Men worked outside the home in cities and children had no economic role. Men saw their children less frequently but when they saw them it was more likely for entertainment than for work. As a result of all these factors, the American family changed significantly.

c.   The birth rate in the American family declined in the late nineteenth century for a number of reasons. In cities (where a constantly increasing percentage of Americans lived) children did not work. Parents began to realize that children, until age 16, were a cost rather than an addition to income. Women began to feel more responsibility for their children's health. With more care required for each child, there was pressure to limit the number of children. Americans also turned more toward entertainment and luxury items. Reducing the number of children was one way to save money to buy these items.

d.   The birth rate in the American family declined in the late nineteenth century because more Americans got married, but had fewer children. As the country became more industrialized it was easier for people to marry, since men did not need to own land before they could marry. Also, young people were less controlled by their parents, so they could marry earlier. With more marriages but fewer children, there were more families, but they were smaller.

10.   List as many effects as you can of the decline in the birth rate in American families in the late nineteenth century. Consider effects on men, women, and children, along with more general social, political, and economic effects.

LESSON 21   Recognizing and Evaluating Types of Reasoning

Q Evaluate the arguments below in terms of their reasoning (cause-and-effect, generalization, or comparison). If an argument contains more than one type of reasoning, focus on the most important type.

1. Immigrant labor led to a larger supply of workers. This allowed factories to lower wages.

2. Workers in America were much better off in the 1940s than they were in the 1890s. Working conditions were better and wages were higher than in the 1890s.

3. Millions of Irish emigrated to the United States from Ireland in the 1840s due to the potato famine in Ireland.

[Continued on next page.]

[Continued from previous page.]

4. Most immigrants settled in ethnic neighborhoods, called ethnic enclaves, where each ethnic group could preserve the customs from its old country.

5. Corrupt urban bosses were a direct result of large-scale immigration in the late 1800s. Since immigrants were largely ignorant of the political system in America, they could easily be manipulated by the bosses who got and kept power.

6. The great number of strikes in the late 1800s show that workers were willing to fight for better pay and better working conditions. But few strikes were successful at that time.

LESSON 22   Identifying and Evaluating Proof and Debating Reasoning

This lesson focuses on two types of reasoning: proof and debating (or eliminating alternatives). Proof reasoning is further broken down into proof by evidence or example, and proof by authority.

You can identify proof by evidence by watching for evidence or factual information that is used to support an argument. You have already learned to evaluate evidence in an argument by using PROP—asking if it is a primary source, if the author of the evidence has a reason to distort, if there is other evidence to support it, and whether it is a public or private statement. The only other question you need to ask of proof by evidence is: "Even if the evidence or information is true, does it actually prove the argument?"

For example, suppose Fred is on trial for theft. If Fred's lawyer presented strong evidence that Fred is kind to dogs, we would still feel that the evidence does not prove that Fred is innocent, since it has little to do with the crime.

You can recognize proof by authority by watching for appeals to a person's expertise, notoriety, or education. You can tell when a person is eliminating alterna-tives in an argument by watching for such cue phrases as "couldn't have been," "must have been," and "but this is wrong because." The key question for this type of reasoning is: "Have all the alternatives been eliminated?"

For example, the prosecuting attorney in a kidnapping case in Oregon might say, "Only Mary and John had a motive to commit the crime, but Mary was in Florida on the date of the crime, so John must have committed it." The important question is whether Mary and John really were the only ones with a motive to commit the crime.

When a person is arguing against an opposing point of view, that person is debating. Does the person summarize the other view fairly and are the criticisms fair?

All of these types of reasoning are explained on pp. 11–14 in the "Guide to Critical Thinking." As you identify and evaluate the items below note especially the key questions in the boxes on pages 11 and 13. Note also the fallacies which will help you notice weaknesses in some items.

 Label each of the following arguments by writing the letter on the line next to it. Then in the space below each item, evaluate it.

    E   The argument illustrates proof by **evidence** or example.

    A   The argument illustrates proof by **authority.**

    D   The argument illustrates **debating** or eliminating alternatives.

_____1.   Medical care in the United States is improving, as shown by government statistics that doctors' salaries are increasing rapidly.

Evaluation

[Continued on next page.]

[Continued from previous page.]

_____2.   Since Pete was not home all summer, he could not have fixed the door.
Marie was the only other person at home besides me, and I didn't fix it. So
Marie must have fixed it.

Evaluation

_____3.   Housing conditions for immigrants in the Chicago Stock Yards District
were deplorable around 1900, as shown by sociology professors
Breckenridge and Abbott in their highly regarded study.

Evaluation

_____4.   According to the Historical Statistics of the United States (published by
the U.S. Government) employment in manufacturing and construction
increased from 4 million to 13 million workers from 1880 to 1920, a larger
percentage increase than any other category of employment.

Evaluation

[Continued on next page.]

[Continued from previous page.]

_____5.   William Graham Sumner argues that poor immigrants deserve to be poor because they do not work hard. But he's wrong. Many immigrants work very hard but cannot get ahead because rich owners oppress them.

Evaluation

_____6.   Senator Granitsas favors Southeastern European immigration to the United States because he's Greek and because he thinks all those new immigrants will eventually vote for him. (Senator Granitsas had made a speech favoring immigration, arguing that immigrants help the country by working hard and bringing new skills.)

Evaluation

_____7.   There is no need to argue whether immigrants have a good effect on neighborhoods. It is common knowledge that they turn neighborhoods into slums.

Evaluation

[Continued on next page.]

[Continued from previous page.]

_____8.   When Henry Frick refused to negotiate and then locked the workers out of the Homestead Plant, he left them no choice but to use force.

Evaluation

_____9.   This book is the best study on the American Federation of Labor up to 1930. The author gathered statistics on membership for every year up to 1930 and she read every biography of the leaders of the AFL.

Evaluation

_____10.   Some extremists argue that we should let all immigrants into the country, while extremists on the other side want to keep everyone out. Obviously the best policy is between these extremes. We should let in half the people who want to come.

Evaluation

LESSON 23   What Were American Cities Like in the Late 1800s?

Part 1

 Read the information below and use it to decide on the issue:

> On balance, were urban bosses good for American cities in the late 1800s?

1. American cities grew very rapidly from 1865 to 1900. Some cities grew more than 10 times as big in 35 years. One city grew 70 times as large.

2. A political boss was the political leader of a city. Sometimes he was the mayor. Sometimes he held a minor post in city government (such as street superintendent) or was not an official at all. But he always controlled the mayor and the city government.

3. The city boss controlled a political machine, an organization to make sure people voted for the boss's candidates, an organization to make sure the boss remained in political control. (Glaab 1967, page 204 and Cornwell 1970, page 135—See the sources beginning on p. 165 for the full listing of sources.)

4. The bosses provided immigrants with services. They helped immigrants find jobs and places to live, helped them become citizens, and gave them financial aid in times of need. (Bruner 1972, 180)

5. The bosses were freely elected. No one was forced to vote for them. So, if they were not providing the needed services to the city's residents they would have been voted out. (Cornwell 1970, 137)

6. The bosses controlled city offices so they could put in their friends and cronies. Bosses gave immigrants jobs in exchange for the immigrants' votes (called patronage) and a portion of their salaries. According to an investigation in 1839, Tammany Hall (which Boss Tweed later controlled) got people jobs on the New York Customs staff. In return the people gave Tammany part of their salary. (Glaab 1967, 204)

7. Bosses cut through bureaucratic red tape and got things done. Boss Tweed provided New York City with an efficient machine, and people stated that under Boss Sheppard, Washington, D.C. was becoming "cleaner and more attractive." (Glaab 1967, 210) Without the boss around there was constant fighting between officials, and nothing got done. (Wade 1971, 134)

8. In New York City under Boss Tweed, new streets were laid, the park system was expanded, and the transportation system was improved. (Bruner 1972, 179)

9. Whatever improvements were made in New York City under Tweed were made

[Continued on next page.]

[Continued from previous page.]

at a very stiff price. (Bruner 1972, 179) He stole about $45 million from the taxpayers of New York City. He also saw to it that taxes for his friends and supporters were reduced. (Cornwell 1970, 136)

10. In a New York City election in 1844 with Tammany Hall in control, 55,000 votes were cast—10,000 more than the number of residents eligible to vote. Boss Tweed was in power in the 1860s. (*Dictionary of American Biography*, p. 80)

11. The Tweed Ring stole most of its money by overcharging the taxpayers on every job, every service. (For example, the Ring passed a rule that everyone charging the city for a product or service must charge 85% more than the actual cost for the product or service.) The Tweed Ring simply paid back part of the overcharge to the person performing the service and kept the rest. (*Dictionary of American Biography*, p. 81)

12. Patronage jobs may have looked bad, but it allowed the government to work in harmony since all the workers owed allegiance and knew the boss.

13. The Brooklyn Bridge, which improved transportation in the area, was begun under Boss Tweed. (*Dictionary of American Biography*, p. 80)

14. The middle class and newspapers were very critical of the bosses. For example, newspaper cartoonist Thomas Nast criticized Boss Tweed. (*Dictionary of American Biography*, p. 81)

15. Political Boss George Washington Plunkitt said in response to the criticism that he stole city money by using inside information, "Ain't it perfectly honest to charge a good price and make a profit on my investment and foresight? Of course it is." (Bruner 1972, 180)

16. Naturally the newspapers complained about the bosses. The newspapers were controlled by the upper middle class who were upset when taxes got higher than the graft they received. (Wade 1971, 134)

17. In 1872 the Tweed Ring was driven out of power by the bankers because all the stealing and corruption drove down the city's credit rating. (Glaab 1967)

18. If Tweed was popular then he should have been elected himself, not have worked behind the scenes.

Part II

 Read the information below and use it to decide on the issue:

On balance, were American cities healthy places to live in the late 1800s?

19. American cities grew rapidly between 1865 and 1900.

[Continued on next page.]

[Continued from previous page.]

20. According to Jacob Riis, a photographer and journalist in New York City, 300,000 people lived in a square mile. Over 75,000 per square mile is considered unhealthy today. (Wade 1971, 138)

21. Cities in the late 1800s were healthy compared to the early 1800s. According to the American Heart Association, in 1872 filtered water and immunization had cut typhoid dramatically. (Bruner 1972, 174–75)

22. By 1910, 70% of cities owned their own waterworks. This public water supply allowed them to pipe clean water to city residents. Sewers were in separate pipes. Indoor plumbing was much more sanitary. (Schultz 1978, 133)

23. In cities, 70% of trolleys were still horse drawn in 1890. Horse droppings all over the streets contaminated the water supply causing dysentery. (Bruner 1972, 174 and Wade 1979, 137)

24. A Congressional investigation in New York City in 1900 said that conditions in the tenements were worse than in 1850. The air shafts bred rats and other rodents. (Wade 1971, 279)

25. Incandescent lights were used in the late 1800s in cities. They were safer than kerosene or coal so they cut the risk of fire and they illuminated the street, thereby reducing crime. (Bruner 1972, 174)

26. Crime, fires, and disease were all serious problems in cities in the late 1800s. People still heated with coal which was a fire hazard. Pollution from industries also lowered people's life expectancies. (Wade 1979, 137–38)

27. In the late 1800s fewer horses were used for pulling trollies, so the amount of horse droppings was reduced. (Green 1965, 119)

28. In 1872 the American Health Association said that disease was still a serious problem. (Schultz 1978, 131)

29. Where improvements were made they were only done in the rich areas of the cities. For example, plumbing was rare in the poor areas of the city. (Statement by Jane Addams about Chicago in Bruner, page 158)

30. Mortality from typhoid dropped 65% by 1907. (Schultz 1978, 134)

31. In the late 1800s streets were paved which reduced health problems from mud and wooden streets. (Glaab 1967, 27)

32. In the 1860s and 1870s water supplies were sometimes contaminated by the overflow from privies (toilets). (Schultz 1978, 134)

33. Cities instituted inspection of meat and dairy products in the late 1800s. (Glaab 1967, 25)

Sources

Bruner, James E. *Industrialism: The American Experience.* Beverly Hills, CA: Benziger, 1972.

[Continued on next page.]

[Continued from previous page.]

Cornwell, Elmer E., Jr. "Political Bosses and the Newcomers," in *Cities and City Life*, edited by Helen MacGill Hughes. Boston: Allyn and Bacon, 1970.

Glaab, Charles N. and A. Theodore Brown. *A History of Urban America*. New York: Macmillan, 1967.

Green, Constance McLaughlin, *The Rise of Urban America*. New York: Harper & Row, 1965.

Malone, Dumas, ed. "William Marcy Tweed." In *Dictionary of American Biography*, Volume X. New York: Scribner's, 1936.

Schultz, Stanley K. and Clay McShane. "To Engineer the Metropolis: Sewers, Sanitation and City Planning in Late Nineteenth Century America," *Journal of American History*, 65 (September 1978), pp. 389–411.

Tweed, William Marcy. *Dictionary of American Biography*, Volume X, edited by Dumas Malone. New York: Scribner's, 1936.

Wade, Richard C. "The American City: Whence and Whither," *American Heritage*, February/March 1979.

Wade, Richard C. *Cities in American Life*. Boston: Houghton Mifflin, 1971.

LESSON 24   What Was the Town of Pullman Like?

In the 1880s George Pullman built a model town near Chicago for his Pullman Palace Car Company workers. He named the town Pullman. The two interpretations below give different views of what the town was like.

Interpretation A

(1)   The Pullman Strike of 1894 was a major event in American labor history. The railway workers, backed by Eugene V. Debs and the American Railway Union (ARU), were crushed by George Pullman who was backed by the power of the United States government. How did this important strike come about?

(2)   The owner of the Pullman Palace Car Company, George Pullman, started the so-called "model town" for his workers in the 1880s. Pullman said the town was to benefit his workers. In reality, the town was begun so Pullman could make money and better control his workers. For example, Pullman bought water for $.04 per 1,000 gallons and sold it to the renters in town for $.10 per 1,000 gallons. The town charged residents $2.25 per 1,000 cubic feet for natural gas which the company paid $.33 to make. In Chicago people paid $1.00–$1.25 for gas. The rents in the town were 15%–20% higher for worse apartments than in neighboring towns.[1] It is well to remember that Pullman had a monopoly on the services in the town, so it makes sense that he would collect unusually large profits. He made a handsome 8% profit per year on the town.[2]

(3)   Pullman used the town to control the employees in several ways. Although not all the workers in the Pullman Company lived in the "model" town, Pullman exerted a great deal of pressure on the workers to live in the town. Workers who did not live in the town were laid off or fired first during bad times.[3] Once they moved into the town workers were powerless. Pullman appointed the town officials, had the rents deducted from paychecks before giving the checks to the workers, controlled the businesses and newspaper (*The Pullman Journal*) in town and had a spy system set up.[4] During the strike, the newspaper never wavered from pro-company position, the businesses would give no credit to the strikers, the town would not allow strikers to rent or use the "public" halls, and the town eventually evicted (threw out) the strikers.[5]

(4)   Living conditions for the workers in the town were poor. The "blocks" were slums where the apartments were crowded and some families had to pass through other apartments to get to their own.[6] Some of the facilities in the tenements were restricted—only one water faucet for each group of five families, and the same toilet for two or more families.[7] These terrible conditions and the complete control over the residents of the town by George Pullman led one worker to say:

> We are born in a Pullman house, fed from the Pullman shop, taught in the Pullman school, catechized in the Pullman church, and when we die, we shall be buried in the Pullman cemetery and go to Pullman hell.[8]

(5)   The situation in the "model town"

[Continued on next page.]

Interpretation A

[Continued from previous page.]

was bad enough. When a depression hit in 1893, Pullman laid off (let go) more than 3,000 of his 5,800 employees. Then he cut wages by 25%–40% but kept the rents the same in the town. The results were disastrous. Very few workers had more than six dollars a week left after the company had made its deductions for food, rent, and other charges. In one case a worker found that his net earnings for the week came to two cents.[9] Pullman claimed he had to cut wages to keep the company in business, and yet through the entire time period he kept paying 8% dividends to the company stockholders.[10] His hypocrisy was plain to see, so the workers secretly joined the American Railway Union and then went to talk with Pullman.

(6) Mr. Pullman refused to negotiate with the workers and the next day three of the union negotiators were laid off.[11] The union still did not strike, and tried to talk with Pullman once more. Again, Pullman refused to negotiate,[12] so the bloody Pullman Strike of 1894 began.

Endnotes for Interpretation A

[1] Testimony by Reverend William H. Carwardine of the Pullman Methodist Episcopal Church to the United States Strike Commission Report, Senate Executive Document No. 7 (53rd Congress, 3rd Session), August 17, 1894:

> "The water tax has always been a burden upon the people. Bought [by the Pullman Company] under contract for 4 cents per 1,000 gallons, it was retailed [sold] to the tenant for 10 cents per 1,000 gallons..."

[2] *The Chicago Times*, June 20, 1894:

> "The company gets a great income from their tenants. I am told it amounts to 8 per cent per annum [year] on the investment."

[3] Extracts from the Report of the Commissioners, The State Bureau of Labor Statistics on the Industrial, Social, and Economic Conditions of Pullman, Illinois in the appendix to: Mrs. Duane Doty, *The Town of Pullman*, Pullman, Illinois: T.P. Struhsacker, 1893:

> "The general management at Pullman of course partakes of the sentiment of its founder—a broad, comprehensive humanitarian...[i]f one of two men must be discharged [fired], and each has a family, and one resides away from Pullman and the other at Pullman, the resident [of Pullman] is to be preferred [to keep his job]."

[4] Milton Meltzer (historian), *Bread and Roses: The Struggle of American Labor, 1865–1915*. New York, Random House, 1967, p. 150.

[5] *The Chicago Times*, May 15, 1894:

> "Saturday Mr. Parend [Assistant Superintendent of the town] made the somewhat startling announcement that those who are in arrears of rent and on strike would have to move out."

[6] *The Chicago Times*, June 20, 1894. Quote by an unidentified gentleman who lived for years in Pullman:

> "My people live away up in the attic, as they do in the stifling quarters of New York, and as that part of the block wasn't intended for use in that way and no preparation made for it, the family on the top floor has to pass through the apartments of the family on the second [floor] in order to secure ingress [entrance] and egress [exit]."

[7] Almont Lindsey (historian), *The Pullman Strike*. (Chicago, University of Chicago Press, 1942) quoted in Meltzer, *Bread and Roses*, p. 149.

[8] Quoted in Alice Gordon, *The Promise of America*. (Chicago, Science Research Associates, 1970), p. 373.

[Continued on next page.]

Endnotes for Interpretation A

[Continued from previous page.]

9 Reverend William H. Carwardine, quoted in Foster Rhea Dulles (historian), *Labor in America: A History.* (New York, Thomas Y. Crowell, 1968), p. 172.

10 *The Chicago Times*, May 15, 1894:

"Today the Pullman Company will declare a quarterly dividend of 2 percent on its capital stock of $30,000,000 and President George M. Pullman is authority for the statement that his company owes no man a cent. This despite the assertion of Mr. Pullman that the works have been run at a loss for eight months."

11 Meltzer (historian), *Bread and Roses*, p. 152.

12 "Mr. Pullman Talks Freely," *New York Sun*, July 5, 1894:

"We declined to see any committee from the American Railway Union...."

"Mr. Pullman's Statement," *New York Tribune*, July 14, 1894:

Headline: "THERE WAS NOTHING TO ARBITRATE—DEMANDS MADE BY THE WORKMEN WERE UNREASONABLE"

Interpretation B

(1) One of the important events in American labor history was the Pullman Strike of 1894. Historians have studied many aspects of the strike, such as the problem of government intervention into labor-management disputes. One aspect of the strike which deserves close study is how the whole thing began.

(2) The owner of the Pullman Palace Car Company, George Pullman, started a model town to benefit his workers (and thereby draw better workers to his company), and to serve as an example to other companies of how to uplift workers.[1] Some people have alleged that Pullman made excessive profits on the services in the town. This is not true. For example, Pullman made only $30.86 per month profits for water for the whole town.[2] When the rate for water went up to 6.8 cents per 1,000 gallons, the town lost $591.07 per month.[3] The town made $1.67 per month per worker in profit from its natural gas sales. This rate was about the same for country towns, so it certainly was not excessive.[4]

(3) The rents in the town were a little higher than surrounding towns, but that was because the apartments and living conditions were better. The mostly modern, brick buildings were:

bordered with bright beds of flowers and green velvety stretches of lawn, shaded with trees, and dotted with parks and pretty water vistas, and glimpses here and there of artistic sweeps of landscape gardening.[5]

(4) Some people have charged that Pullman had total control over the town, but this is not so. Since the town was part of the town of Hyde Park and of Chicago, its aldermen (the leaders of the town) were elected as a part of Chicago. Residents of the town voted by secret ballot, so there was no way for Pullman to control who they elected. One observer of the town heard men freely praising and criticizing company officials, and a bookstore in the town sold a book openly critical of Pullman. Moreover, the stores in town were rented out to anyone, and the other institutions (such as the library and parks) were run by the townspeople, not the company.[6]

(5) Most of the employees of the company did not live in the town, so it

[Continued on next page.]

Interpretation B

[Continued from previous page.]

certainly cannot be said that Pullman forced his employees to live in the town.[7] Thus, some Pullman employees lived in the model town under reasonably good conditions, for reasonable rent, and with some control over the town and the freedom to move out if they desired.

(6) This situation was disrupted by the start of the depression of 1893. Pullman had to lay off several thousand of his workers but was able to keep the company going by taking on work at prices which gave the company no profit. Finally, he had to ask the workers to take a pay cut of 25% to 40%.[8] The pay cut hurt the workers, but without it the whole company would have been closed and all the workers unemployed.

(7) Some people say that Pullman should have cut the rents in the town also. The town was a separate company from the business, however, and it had to be run at a profit separate from the company.[9] The costs of running the town dictated that rents remain the same.

(8) The workers' response to the wage cut was to secretly join the American Railway Union and to come to Mr. Pullman to make demands. Mr. Pullman would have been glad to arbitrate with his own workers, but he could not tolerate the interference of a large union with national labor interests in mind rather than the interests of his own workers.[10] Three of the union men who met with Mr. Pullman were fired the next day. The union ignored the fact that the three workers let go were part of a more general lay off (there were 43 men on the committee that met with Mr. Pullman), and charged Pullman with firing the workers because they were in the union.[11] On this false charge, the union voted to strike and shut down the Pullman factory. The great Pullman Strike of 1894 had begun.

Endnotes for Interpretation B

[1] Extracts from the Report of Commissioners, The State Bureau of Labor Statistics on the Industrial, Social, and Economic Conditions of Pullman, Illinois in the appendix to Mrs. Duane Doty, *The Town of Pullman*, Pullman, Illinois: T.P. Struhsacker, 1893.

[2] "The Strike at Pullman: Statements of George M. Pullman and 2nd Vice-President T.H. Wickes." Statement by Mr. Wickes:

"This percentage, $86.71, added to the amount paid the village [Hyde Park] for the water supply to the tenants per month, brings the cost to the company to $975.18 per month, which is less than the average amount, $1006.04, charged to tenants, by the insignificant sum of $30.86. It would be difficult to have a more exact agreement, and the facts thus show that Mr. Carwardine's statement that the company was charging the tenants 2 1/2 times the cost of the water was utterly reckless and untrue."

[3] Wickes, Ibid.

[4] Wickes, Ibid.

"The average revenue to the company from each wage worker using gas, including foremen, is approximately $1.67 per month....It should be compared with the gas rates of country towns, and it is believed that upon such comparison the Pullman rate will be found to be less than their rates."

[5] Pullman Company pamphlet—description of the town of Pullman. Also, statement by T.H. Wickes, and Extracts from the Report of Commissioners.

[6] Charles H. Eaton, *Pullman and Paternalism.*

[7] "The Strike at Pullman," statement by George Pullman.

[Continued on next page.]

Endnotes for Interpretation B
[Continued from previous page.]

8   "Mr. Pullman's Statement," *The New York Times*, July 14, 1894:

"The great business depression existing throughout the country had naturally resulted in a wage depression, and the only hope of getting orders was by bidding for work at prices as low as, or lower than, could be made by other shops, and this, of course, necessitated a reduction in the wages of the employees at Pullman."

9   "Mr. Pullman's Statement," Ibid.:

"The average rental of tenements at Pullman is at the rate of $3 a room a month, and the renting of houses at Pullman has no relation to the work in the shops....In short, the renting business of the Pullman Company is governed by the same conditions which govern any other large owner of real estate....It can hardly be asked that the Pullman Company alone should abandon the ordinary rules which govern [the real estate business]."

10 "Mr. Pullman's Statement," Ibid.:

"In the early part of May, a committee of the employees demanded a restoration of the wages of a year ago. I explained to this committee minutely and laboriously the facts, showing that the company was already paying them more than it was receiving for their contract work and I offered them, for complete assurance, and to end all questions, an inspection of our books and contracts in hand.

"How could I, as president of the Pullman Company, consent to agree that if any body of men [the union] not concerned with the interests of the company's shareholders should, as arbitrators, for any reason seeming good to them so decree, I would open the shops, employ workmen at wages greater than their work could be sold for, and continue this ruinous policy indefinitely; or be accused of a breach of faith?

"[The real] question was as to the possibility of the creation and duration of a dictatorship [of the union] which could make all the industries of the United States...hostages for the granting of any fantastic whim of such a dictator."

11 Statement by Mr. Wickes. From "The Strike at Pullman":

"Testimony has been given before the commission that the immediate cause of the strike was the discharge of three employees contrary to the assurance I had given to the committee of workmen that none of them should be affected by serving on the committee. I gave such assurance upon request, and with entire willingness, and it was not violated, and no such complaint was ever made, I think, to any official of the company. There were forty-three members of the committee at the conference on May 9, and on May 10 it happened that in temporarily "laying off" men for whom there was no immediate work, three men were included who were said to be on the committee, as to each of whom the subordinate officials concerned deny that they at the time knew he was on the committee and say that the laying off was caused by nothing but the ordinary course of business."

 Interpretation A

1.   What is the main point of Interpretation A?

2.   What is the unstated assumption in paragraph 3, sentence 6?

[Continued on next page.]

[Continued from previous page.]

3. For each of the paragraphs listed in the table below, fill in the types of reasoning, key question(s), and how well Interpretation A answers the key question(s).

Paragraph	Type of Reasoning	Key Question(s)	Your Evaluation (How well answered— Any fallacies?)
Paragraph 2, sentences 3–7			
Paragraph 2, sentence 8			
Paragraph 4, sentence 2 (including endnote 6)			
Paragraph 5, sentence 7 (including endnote 10)			
Paragraph 6			

[Continued on next page.]

[Continued from previous page.]
4.   Evaluate the evidence in endnote 5.

 Interpretation B

5.   What is the main point of Interpretation B?

6.   What is the unstated assumption in paragraph 4, sentence 3?

[Continued on next page.]

[Continued from previous page.]

7. For each of the paragraphs listed in the table below, fill in the types of reasoning, key question(s), and how well Interpretation B answers the key question(s).

Paragraph	Type of Reasoning	Key Question(s)	Your Evaluation (How well answered— Any fallacies?)
Paragraph 2			
Paragraph 6			
Paragraph 7			
Paragraph 8, sentences 3–4 (including endnote 11)			

[Continued on next page.]

[Continued from previous page.]

8.   Evaluate the evidence in endnote 8.

Q   General Questions

9.   Compare the evidence in endnote 1 from Interpretation A with the evidence in endnote 2 from Interpretation B. Which is stronger?

10.   Compare the evidence in endnote 6 from Interpretation A with the evidence in endnote 5 from Interpretation B. Which is stronger?

11.   Compare the evidence in endnote 12 from Interpretation A with the evidence in endnote 10 from Interpretation B. Which is stronger?

[Continued on next page.]

[Continued from previous page.]

 Subquestions on the Town of Pullman

Evaluate the evidence presented to answer each of the following questions.

12. Were water and gas prices in the town fair?

13. Were rents in town reasonable given living conditions?

14. Was Pullman justified in cutting wages while keeping rents the same?

15. Did Pullman control what happened in town like a dictator or did the towns-people run the town free from Pullman's control?

16. Did Pullman or the union provoke the strike?

LESSON 25   Should the United States Restrict Immigration?

Background Information

America has always drawn a high level of immigration, but the greatest period was between 1870 and 1920. In fact, the period from 1890 to 1915 is known as the Great Migration. One of the characteristics of this migration was an increase of immigrants from Southern Europe (Italy, Greece, Yugoslavia, etc.) and Eastern Europe (Poland, Lithuania, Russia, etc.). Previous periods of immigration had been dominated by newcomers from Northern and Western Europe, especially England,

Ireland, Germany, and Scandinavia.

Some Americans wanted to restrict this new immigration. Others agreed with Emma Lazarus' famous phrase: "Give me your tired, your poor, your huddled masses yearning to breathe free, the wretched refuse of your teaming shore." These two perspectives on immigration are represented by the arguments below. The arguments focus on immigration from roughly 1870 to 1920.

Relevant Information

A. In general, unskilled jobs yield lower wages than skilled jobs.

B. Crime rates are generally much higher among men than women.

C. When workers get lower wages, there may be a greater demand for workers, which might lower the unemployment rate.

D. All people consume goods and services, which generally increases the demand for those goods and services, which leads to increased production of those goods and services, which generally leads to increased employment.

E. Crimes are generally committed by adults, not children.

F. Most immigrants received unskilled jobs.

G. Most immigrants to the United States were adult men without wives or children.

Historian A

(1) Into this favored section of the earth's surface have been introduced ever-increasing numbers of the lower classes of foreign nations. What has been their effect upon the standard of living (the measure of how well off people are economically) of people in the United States?

(2) Immigrants come from countries which have a lower standard of living than in the United States. Common observations and general testimony es-

tablish this beyond the need of proof. If they did not have a lower standard of living, very few of our immigrants would come here, for, as we have seen, the major reason they come to America is to raise their standard of living. It is significant, however, that as time goes on, the bulk of immigration has been recruited from more and more backward races of Europe.

[Continued on next page.]

Historian A

[Continued from previous page.]

(3) As a result, immigrants work for lower wages than do Americans. This lowers the wages of American workers. Some people argue that the immigrants push American-born workers up to higher-level jobs. The fallacy in this is that while a few American workers move to higher-level positions, most stay at the same jobs for lower pay. Some American-born workers do not get jobs at all. Thus, immigrants cause higher unemployment among American workers.

(4) Immigrants also have a negative effect on unions. They work for lower wages, which breaks union bargaining power, and they are used as strikebreakers. Some people argue that American workers are better off than they were fifty years ago. The key question is not whether the workers have more, but how they are doing compared to other groups, and compared to how they would be doing without the immigrants.

(5) One of the chief objections to unrestricted immigration is the increase in pauperism (poverty)[1] and crime[2] caused by immigrants. A nation which has increasing numbers of people who are ill-housed, ill-clothed, and ill-fed is worse off. The paupers add to the burden of welfare to take care of them,[3] and the criminals cost everyone. As a result of the careful studies by the Immigration Commission, this is one of the very few effects of immigration about which we may feel justified in setting down definite conclusions.

(6) Still another way in which immigrants become a burden upon the American public is through insanity. Many are screened out by immigration officials, but large numbers later appear in the category of the insane. The 1908 Report of the Commissioner General of Immigration calculated that about 30% of the insane are foreign-born.[4] The Commission concluded, "For the high ratio of insanity among the foreign-born...it is probably true that racial traits or tendencies have a more or less important influence. A further cause of mental disease is probably to be found in the total change in climate, occupation, and habits of life which the majority of immigrants experience after arrival in the United States."

(7) In sum, we cannot escape the fact that the United States is not prepared to accept the tremendous responsibility of admitting unlimited numbers of aliens to our shores. Immigration must be restricted.

Endnotes for Historian A

[1] The *Special Report of the Census Bureau on Paupers in Almshouses, 1904* showed that in 1903 immigrants were 13.4% of the population; they made up about 40% of the paupers (poor people) in almshouses (a home for people too poor to support themselves).

[2] Laughlin Report, Survey on Crime:

Based on the number of immigrants in the United States, the recent immigrants from Southern and Eastern Europe (Serbia, Spain, Bulgaria, Poland, Turkey, Italy, Greece, Portugal, and so forth) have a crime rate much higher than their percentage of the population. For example, Serbia has a crime rate fourteen times her population in the United States. There seems to be something in the racial character of some of our immigrants which causes them to commit crimes.

[3] Mr. Prescott F. Hall published an estimate that the total yearly cost of caring for the foreign-born of New York state alone is $12 million.

[Continued on next page.]

Endnotes for Historian A
[Continued from previous page.]

[4] The percentage of foreign-born insane persons is even higher according to records kept by hospitals. In 1903 the percentage was 34.3% in the United States as a whole and 63.4% at Bellevue and Allied Hospitals.

Historian B

(1) One of the most persistent economic fallacies in popular thought (made by Historian A) is the notion that immigrants take jobs away from American-born workers. This rests on the mistaken belief that only a fixed number of jobs exist in any economy and that any newcomer threatens the job of an old resident. Actually, the number of jobs expands with an expanding population. Statistics prove this point. From 1870, when immigration began to assume important proportions, to 1930 the population rose from 38.5 million to 112.8 million people or about 200%. The number of gainfully-employed people increased, however, from 12.5 million in 1870 to 48.8 million in 1930, or nearly 300%.

(2) Immigrants did not take many jobs from American-born workers. They set up whole new categories of employment, such as the Chinese laundry and the Greek sponge industry. They started a demand for products from their native countries, which helped our import/export industries. Moreover, over 50% of immigrants wrote "no occupation" on their forms—they were women, children, and older people. Those Americans, such as in the steel or textile industries, who were replaced in jobs by immigrants generally moved up to supervisory positions. This upward mobility is the hallmark of American social democracy.

(3) Opposition to immigrants was sometimes based on the grounds that it tended to lower the American standard of living. Many of the problems associated with this time period around 1900, however, were really a result of rapid industrialization. Immigrants played only a small part in this whole development. The United States Immigration Commission tended to throw some blame upon the immigrant population for low wages and other evils. It concluded that immigrants tended to undercut the wages of native-born workers, because immigrants, on a whole, received lower wages than American-born workers. The Commission overlooked the fact, however, that immigrants received the lowest wages because they took unskilled jobs.

(4) The Commission also said that immigrants were holding back labor's advance because they were difficult to unionize. Actually, this was due to the fact that immigrants were in unskilled industries which were not unionized at the time. Also, eventually immigrants did join unions in large numbers.

(5) No one has been able to show that immigrants hurt our country. And immigration definitely improves the lot of those who come to our shores. Therefore, immigration should not be restricted.

[Continued on next page.]

[Continued from previous page.]

 Historian A

1. What is the main point of Historian A?

2. Evaluate one of the arguments in the second paragraph.

3. Evaluate the first two sentences in the third paragraph.

4. Evaluate the last two sentences in the third paragraph.

5. Evaluate the argument on pauperism in paragraph five.

[Continued on next page.]

[Continued from previous page.]

6.   Evaluate the argument on crime in paragraph five.

7.   What assumption does the Commission make in the sixth paragraph?

 Historian B

8.   What is the main point of Historian B?

9.   Identify and evaluate the type of reasoning in the first two sentences in the first paragraph.

10.   Evaluate the reasoning in the last two sentences in the first paragraph.

[Continued on next page.]

[Continued from previous page.]

11. Evaluate the argument in the fifth sentence of the second paragraph.

12. Evaluate the reasoning in the first three sentences of the third paragraph.

13. Evaluate the reasoning in the last three sentences of the third paragraph.

⬛Q General Questions

14. Which viewpoint, Historian A or Historian B, do you think is stronger? Explain why you think so.

[Continued on next page.]

 ©1991 Midwest Publications/Critical Thinking Press & Software, P.O. Box 448, Pacific Grove, CA 93950

[Continued from previous page.]
Circular Flow Diagram

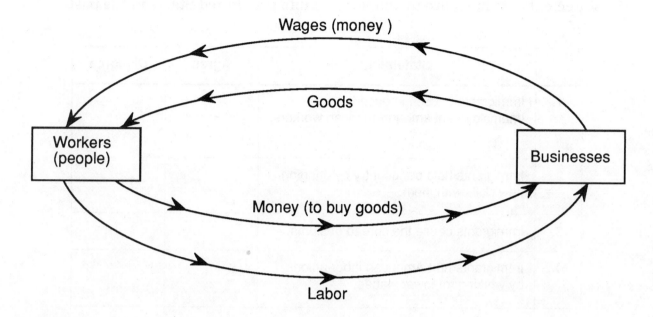

Start at the **People** section of the diagram. Following the bottom arrow, the people, as workers, give their labor to the **Businesses** which pay the workers in the form of wages (top arrow). The **People**, as consumers, take their money to the **Businesses** and buy goods in return.

Let's suppose there are 100 workers in the whole economy, that each worker makes $1.00 per week, that there are two businesses which employ (hire) a total of 100 workers and which make 100 goods per week, costing $1.00 for each good. Thus, there is no unemployment in this economy (all 100 workers are employed).

If 50 workers left the economy, some changes would occur. First, since there is a shortage of workers, the 50 workers who are left might be able to get higher wages. Second, however, since there are 50 fewer consumers, the demand for goods would go down, the businesses would make fewer goods and so the businesses would need fewer workers. The workers might not get a pay raise after all.

 Now suppose that 50 workers were added to the economy. In the space below, describe what would happen. It would be nearly opposite to what was described in the paragraph above. Just start with the workers and follow what would happen from there.

Survey on Immigration

For each of the following statements, check whether you agree or disagree. All the statements are in regard to immigration into the United States in the past 15 years.

	Statement	Agree	Disagree
1.	Immigrants cause increased unemployment among American workers.		
2.	Immigrants help our country by bringing new skills with them.		
3.	Immigrants cause the spread of slums.		
4.	Immigrants hurt American labor unions by working for lower wages.		
5.	Illegal immigrants should be prevented from coming into our country.		
6.	Immigrants are a drain on our country by living on welfare.		
7.	Immigration helps immigrants improve their lives.		
8.	Immigrants blend in easily with American culture.		

©1991 Midwest Publications/Critical Thinking Press & Software, P.O. Box 448, Pacific Grove, CA 93950

LESSON 26   Why Was the Immigration Act of 1924 Passed?

 Examine Documents A–E and the relevant information that follows, then write a minimum 100-word explanation of the factors that probably influenced Congress to pass the Immigration Act of 1924. Mention at least four of the documents in your answer. One part of your answer must explain why the date for figuring the quota was changed from 1910 to 1890, as mentioned in Document A. The reason for the date change can be figured out from the graphs in Document B and the relevant information.

Document A

The "Immigration Act of 1924"...supplants the so-called quota limit act of May 19, 1921, [which] provided that the number of aliens of any nationality admissible to the United States in any fiscal year should be limited to 3 percent of the number of persons of such nationality who were residents in the United States according to the census of 1910....Under the Act of 1924 the number of each nationality who may be admitted annually is limited to 2 percent of the population of such nationality resident in the United States according to the census of 1890....

U.S. Bureau of Immigration, *Annual Report of the Commissioner General of Immigration, 1924.*

Document B

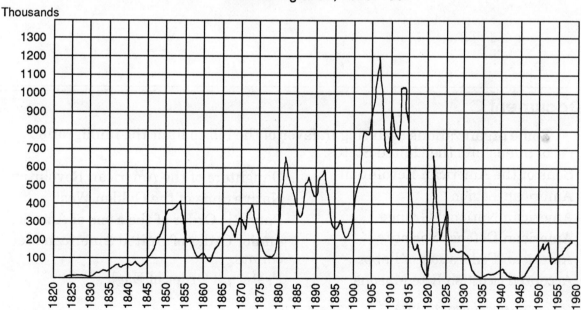

Total Immigration, 1820–1957

From United States Bureau of the Census, *Historical Statistics of the United States, Colonial Times to 1957*, 1960.

[Continued on next page.]

Document B

[Continued from previous page.]

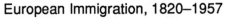

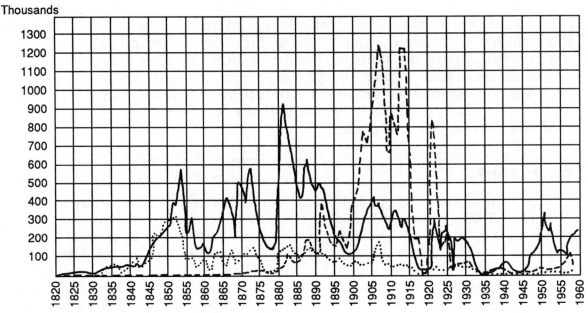

European Immigration, 1820–1957

.... Ireland

——— Northern Europe—Great Britain, Scandinavia, Germany, and Other Northwestern

----- Southern and Eastern European—Poland, Russia, Baltic States, Italy, Other Eastern, and Other Southern

---

Document C

Some organizations declaring in favor of the bill to limit the immigration of aliens into the United States:

Sons of the American Revolution

American Legion

American National Grange

American Defense Society

American Federation of Labor

Accepted Scottish Rite Masons

Daughters of the American Revolution

Native Sons of the Golden West

Patriotic Order of the Sons of America

Junior Order of United American Merchants

Fraternal Order of Eagles

The Congressional Record, 1924.

[Continued on next page.]

[Continued from previous page.]

Document D

I think we now have sufficient population in our country for us to shut the door and to breed up a pure, unadulterated American citizenship. I recognize that there is a dangerous lack of distinction between people of a certain nationality and the breed of a dog....It is the breed of the dog in which I am interested. I would like the members of the Senate to read that book just recently published by Madison Grant, *The Passing of the Great Race*. Thank God we have in America perhaps the largest percentage of any country in the world of pure unadulterated Anglo-Saxon stock; certainly the greatest of any nation in the Nordic breed. It is for the preservation of that splendid stock that has characterized us that I would make this not an asylum for the oppressed of all countries, but a country to assimilate and perfect that splendid type of manhood that has made America the foremost Nation in her progress and in her power, and yet the youngest of all nations. I myself believe that the preservation of her institutions depends upon us now taking counsel with our condition and our experience during the last World War.

Without offense, but with regard to the salvation of our own, let us shut the door....

From an address by Senator Ellison D. Smith, (D-South Carolina), April 9, 1924.

Document E

Morgan in the *Philadelphia Inquirer*, 1919. Historical Pictures Service, Chicago.

[Continued on next page.]

[Continued from previous page.]
Document F

Spoiling the Broth

Gale in the *Los Angeles Times*, 1921.
Historical Pictures Service, Chicago.

Document G

Our study of the army tests of foreign-born individuals has pointed at every step to the conclusion that the **average intelligence of our immigrants is declining**...[as] the migration of the Alpine and Mediterranean races [from southern and eastern Europe] has increased....The representatives of the Alpine and Mediterranean races in our immigration are intellectually inferior to the representatives of the Nordic race [from northern and western Europe] which formerly made up about 50% of our immigration....

From Carl C. Brigham, *A Study of American Intelligence*, 1923.

Relevant Information

1. In 1917 the Bolsheviks (Communists) took over the Russian government.

2. Americans were frightened by the Communist Revolution in Russia. In 1920–21 this fear led to a Red Scare in which large numbers of Communists were rounded up and deported back to their old country.

3. Many Americans believed immigrants from Southern and Eastern Europe were racially inferior to immigrants from Northern and Western Europe.

4. The Sons and Daughters of the American Revolution, the American Legion, the American Defense Society, the Patriotic Order of the Sons of America, and the Fraternal Order of Eagles were all patriotic organizations.

5. Many Americans were afraid of the philosophy of anarchy, which they associated with Communism.

LESSON 27   What Does the Omaha Platform Show about the Populists?

Background Information

The Populist Party of the 1890s was made up of farmers. It first ran candidates for president and other national offices in the election of 1892.

In order to organize for an election and in order to nominate (choose) candidates to run for office, political parties hold conventions. Conventions also write party platforms which state the party's positions on a number of issues. For example, in a platform a party might state that it:

• Opposes gun control;

• Favors a new tax law to reduce taxes;

• Favors putting more United States troops into a certain country;

• Opposes arms talk with our enemies;

• Favors more government help for business;

and so forth.

A party platform can tell us something about the party and its positions. Read the Omaha Platform written by the Populists at their convention in Omaha, Nebraska in 1892 and then answer the questions that your teacher gives you.

The Omaha Platform

Summary of the original platform.

We meet (in Omaha) as our nation is on the verge of moral, political, and material ruin. The rich and the bankers control the money in the country for their own greed. Our present system has led to two classes—tramps and millionaires.

We have seen for more than a quarter of a century the struggles of the two great political parties (the Democrats and Republicans) for power and plunder (theft, robbery). Meanwhile terrible wrongs have been inflicted on the suffering people. Both parties have allowed these dreadful wrongs to develop without any effort to prevent them. The two major parties are dominated by greed, corruption, and rich people.

We declare therefore,

I. Labor forces are hereby united to uplift mankind.

II. Wealth belongs to him who creates it (the workers, not the owner).

III. The industrial worker and the farmer have the same interests and the same enemies.

IV. The people should own the railroads through the government.

V. The government alone, not the bankers, should control the money supply.

VI. There should be free and unlimited coinage of silver in a ratio of 16 to 1 compared to gold. (Gold would be worth 16 times what silver is worth.)

[Continued on next page.]

The Omaha Platform

[Continued from previous page.]

VII. There should be a graduated income tax. (As income goes up, the tax rate goes up. For example, if you make $10,000 you might pay 5%, or $500; if you make $20,000 you might pay 10%, or $2,000. You pay a larger share of a larger income.)

VIII. The government should own and operate the telephone and telegraph (the carriers of information) in the interests of the people.

IX. The land, including the natural resources in the land, belongs to the people. It should not be controlled by speculators (people who buy something expecting to sell it at an unusually large profit), and aliens (non-citizen foreigners) should not be able to own it. Land owned by aliens and railroads should be reclaimed by the government and held for actual settlers.

X. The government should limit immigration into the United States.

XI. There should be a shorter work week for laborers.

XII. The secret ballot should be used in all elections.

XIII. The people should be able to use the initiative (by which private individuals could propose laws) and referendum (on which citizens could express an opinion on an issue by voting on it).

XIV. Senators should be elected directly by the people. (At this time, U.S. Senators were elected by state legislatures, not by citizens directly.)

XV. The President of the United States should be able to serve one four-year term only.

Relevant Information

A. Free coinage of silver would have increased the supply of money. An increase in the supply of money would generally lead to inflation (higher prices), unless the supply of goods and services increased as much.

B. Farmers had tried several times to use the government to regulate (control) the railroads in the interest of the farmers.

C. People who owe money (debtors) generally benefit from inflation. This is because the amount of money they have to repay remains fixed (let's say $100 per year) while their income from selling goods or services generally rises with inflation (let's say from $150 in the first year to $160 in the second year).

D. People who are owed money (creditors—often banks) generally dislike inflation. This is because they will be paid back a fixed amount of money that will buy fewer goods and services as prices increase.

E. Most Populists were farmers.

F. Many industrial unions opposed immigration into the United States.

[Continued on next page.]

[Continued from previous page.]
Part A

Q The Omaha Platform

Based on the Omaha Platform, put a check next to the statements with which the Populists in 1892 would likely have agreed. Write the reason you checked or did not check the statement. Include the location of supporting statements from the Omaha Platform (statement number(s) or introduction) in your explanation. For example, "Statement III shows the Populists were opposed to this idea."

_____1.   Rich people deserve to keep the money they have.

Reason

_____2.   Immigration is bad for the country.

Reason

_____3.   Speculators hurt other people, such as farmers.

Reason

_____4.   Business owners make an important contribution to creating wealth through the production of goods and services.

Reason

_____5.   There is fraud or intimidation of voters in elections.

Reason

_____6.   Wealth should be more equally divided.

Reason

[Continued on next page.]

[Continued from previous page.]

_____7.   Society can be improved through reform.
Reason

_____8.   The people should have more say in government.
Reason

_____9.   Reform can be achieved through the Democratic and Republican Parties.
Reason

_____10.   Freedom is more important than equality.
Reason

_____11.   An important aspect of history is the struggle between the rich and the poor.
Reason

_____12.   The state legislatures are controlled by the rich people.
Reason

[Continued on next page.]

[Continued from previous page.]

_____13.   It is possible for a conspiracy of a small number of people to control the history of a country for a time.

Reason

_____14.   The government is controlled by the rich—it must be reformed.

Reason

_____15.   Bankers have too much power.

Reason

Part B

Q Based on the Omaha Platform and the relevant information, put a check next to the statements which you think are probably true. Write the reason you checked or did not check each statement. Include the location of supporting statements from the Omaha Platform (statement number(s) or introduction) and from the relevant information in your explanation.

_____16.   Many farmers were debtors (they owed money on loans).

Reason

_____17.   Farmers felt railroads were hurting them.

Reason

[Continued on next page.]

[Continued from previous page.]

_____18.   The Populists were trying to gain the support of industrial workers.

Reason

_____19.   Bankers supported the idea of free coinage of silver.

Reason

_____20.   Populists were conservative—that is, they wanted to go back to earlier days. They were not pushing for innovation and change.

Reason

_____21.   Populists were radical—they were suggesting radical change in our society.

Reason

Part C

 The Populists never elected a candidate to the presidency. Why do you suppose they did not win?

Major Sources Used for Lessons

Lesson 6

Coulter, Merton E. "The South During Reconstruction, 1865–1877," in *A History of the South*, edited by Wendel Stephensen and E. M. Coulter. Baton Rouge: Louisiana University Press, 1947.

Randall, James G. *The Civil War and Reconstruction*. Boston: D.C. Heath, 1937.

Stampp, Kenneth. *The Era of Reconstruction, 1865–1877*. New York: Alfred A. Knopf, 1965.

Lesson 7

Dunning, William A. *Reconstruction, Political and Economic, 1865–1877*. New York: Harper, 1907.

Fleming, Walter L., ed. *Documentary History of Reconstruction*, Vol. 2. New York: McGraw-Hill, 1966, first published 1907.

Foner, Eric. *Reconstruction: America's Unfinished Revolution, 1863–1877*. New York: Harper and Row, 1988.

Stampp, *Era*. (See Stampp, Lesson 6)

Lesson 9

DuBois, Ellen Carol. *Feminism and Suffrage: The Emergence of an Independent Women's Movement in America, 1848–1869*. Ithaca, NY: Cornell University Press, 1978. Chapter 2 "The Fourteenth Amendment and the American Equal Rights Association."

Foner, *Reconstruction*. Chapter 6, Section 3 "The Fourteenth Amendment." (See Foner, Lesson 7)

Griffith, Elisabeth. *In Her Own Right: The Life of Elizabeth Cady Stanton*. New York: Oxford University Press, 1984. Chapter 8 "Revolution and Schism, 1865–70."

Schwartz, Bernard, ed. *The Fourteenth Amendment*. New York: New York University Press, 1970. "Landmarks of Legal Liberty" by William Brennan; "Historical Background of the Fourteenth Amendment" by Henry Steele Commanger.

Smith, Page. *Trial by Fire: A People's History of the Civil War and Reconstruction*, Volume 5. New York: McGraw-Hill, 1982. Chapter 40 "Congressional Reconstruction."

Lesson 12

Hayes, Samuel P. *The Response to Industrialism*. Chicago: University of Chicago Press, 1957.

Lesson 14

Bruner, James E., Jr. *Industrialism: The American Experience*. Beverly Hills, CA: Benziger, 1972. Chapter 1 "Industrial Society, Pro and Con."

Lesson 14 [*continued*]

Fine, Sidney. *Laissez-faire and the General Welfare State: A Study of Conflict in American Thought, 1865–1901.* Ann Arbor, MI: The University of Michigan Press, 1956. Chapters I, II, III, IV, VI, and VII.

Gruver, Rebecca Brooks. *An American History.* Reading, MA: Addison-Wesley, 1976. Chapter 18 "Becoming a Great Industrial Power."

Lesson 15

Horowitz, David and Peter Collier. *The Rockefellers: An American Dynasty.* New York: Holt, Rinehart and Winston, 1976.

Lesson 16

Latham, Earl, ed. *John D. Rockefeller: Robber Baron or Industrial Statesman?* Boston: D.C. Heath, 1949.

Nevins, Allan. *Study in Power: John D. Rockefeller.* 2 volumes. New York: Scribner's, 1953.

Tarbell, Ida. *The History of the Standard Oil Company.* New York: McClure, Phillips and Co., 1904.

Lesson 17

Barrett, James R. "Local History and Social History 'Back of the Yards.'" *Reviews in American History* (March, 1988): 43–48.

Breckenridge, Sophonisba P. and Edith Abbott. "Housing Conditions in Chicago, Ill.: Back of the Yards." *The American Journal of Sociology* Vol. XVI, No. 4 (January, 1911): 433–68.

Brody, David. "Slavic Immigrants in the Steel Mills," in *The Private Side of American History*, Volume II edited by Gary B. Nash. New York: Harcourt Brace Jovanovich, 1975.

Bushnell, Charles J. *The Social Problem at the Chicago Stock Yards.* Chicago: University of Chicago Press, 1902.

Kennedy, J.C. and others. *Wages and Family Budgets in the Chicago Stock-Yards District.* Chicago: University of Chicago Press, 1914.

Neill, Charles P. and James Bronson Reynolds. "Commission Report," 1906.

Sinclair, Upton. *The Jungle.* New York: The New American Library, 1905, 1960.

Thompson, Frank H. *The Jungle, Notes.* Lincoln, NE: Cliff's Notes, 1970.

Lesson 18

Hofstadter, Richard. *The Age of Reform: From Bryan to F.D.R.* New York: Random House, 1955. Chapters IV, V, VI.

Lesson 20

Rosenzweig, Linda W. and Peter N. Stearns. *Themes in Modern Social History.* Pittsburgh, PA: Carnegie-Mellon University Press, 1985. Chapter III "Mature Industrial Society, 1870–1950."

Lesson 23

Bruner, James E. *Industrialism: The American Experience.* Beverly Hills, CA: Benziger, 1972. Chapter 5, "Urbanization."

Cornwell, Elmer E., Jr. "Political Bosses and the Newcomers," in *Cities and City Life,* edited by Helen MacGill Hughes. Boston: Allyn and Bacon, 1970.

Glaab, Charles N. and A. Theodore Brown. *A History of Urban America.* New York: Macmillan, 1967. Chapter 8 "Bosses and Reformers."

Green, Constance McLaughlin, *The Rise of Urban America.* New York: Harper & Row, 1965.

Kuzirian, Eugene and Larry Maderos. *Taking Sides: Clashing Views on Controversial Issues in American History,* Vol. II, Guilford, CT: Dushkin. Issue 7, "Urban America: A Healthy Place to Live by 1900?"

Malone, Dumas. ed. "Tweed, William Marcy." *Dictionary of American Biography,* Volume X. New York: Scribner's, 1936.

Wade, Richard C. *Cities in American Life.* Boston: Houghton Mifflin, 1971. Part III, Chapter 5, "The Heyday of Bossism."

Lesson 24

Meltzer, Milton. *Bread and Roses: The Struggle of American Labor, 1865–1915.* New York: Random House, 1967, Chapter 9 "Rebellion on the Railroads."

Sloan, Irving. *Viewpoints on American Labor.* New York: Random House, 1970. Booklet "Trouble on the Tracks: Documentary Sources on the 1894 Pullman Palace Car Strike."

Lesson 25

Ziegler, Benjamin M., ed. *Immigration: An American Dilemma.* Boston: D.C. Heath, 1953. Chapter 3, "The Immigrant: Social and Economic Problems."

Lesson 26

Document-Based Question from the Advanced Placement Test.

Feder, Bernard. *Viewpoints: USA.* New York: American Book Company, 1972. Chapter 11, "Immigration: Should the Golden Door Be Closed?"

Lesson 27

Hofstadter. (See Hofstadter, Lesson 18)